Single Purpose

A Devotional for Singles

Regal

A Division of Gospel Light
Ventura, California, U.S.A.

Published by Regal Books
A Division of Gospel Light
Ventura, California, U.S.A.
Printed in U.S.A.

Regal Books is a ministry of Gospel Light, an evangelical Christian publisher dedicated to serving the local church. We believe God's vision for Gospel Light is to provide church leaders with biblical, user-friendly materials that will help them evangelize, disciple and minister to children, youth and families.

It is our prayer that this Regal book will help you discover biblical truth for your own life and help you meet the needs of others. May God richly bless you.

For a free catalog of resources from Regal Books/Gospel Light please contact your Christian supplier or call 1-800-4-GOSPEL.

Cover Design by Barbara LeVan Fisher
Interior Design by Britt Rocchio
Edited by Karen Kaufman

Library of Congress Cataloging-in-Publication Data
Wright, H. Norman.
    Single purpose / H. Norman Wright.
        p.   cm.
    Includes index.
    ISBN 0-8307-1924-5 (Hardcover)
    1. Single people—Religious life. I. Title.
    BV4596.S5W75   1997   97-14143
    248.8'4—dc21   CIP

1 2 3 4 5 6 7 8 9 10 11 12 13 14 15 16 17 / 04 03 02 01 00 99 98 97

Rights for publishing this book in other languages are contracted by Gospel Literature International (GLINT). GLINT also provides technical help for the adaptation, translation and publishing of Bible study resources and books in scores of languages worldwide. For further information, contact GLINT, P.O. Box 4060, Ontario, CA 91761-1003, U.S.A., or the publisher.

Contents

Introduction

Is singleness a safe state of being that keeps you from having to risk being fully known by another human being? Is it a dreaded, lonely burdensome lifestyle that prohibits you from achieving all your hopes and desires? Or is your singleness a tool fashioned by God to bring you into a relationship with Himself that is preparing you for loving, knowing and serving Him with your whole life?

Let's walk through the following 90 devotionals together to determine what is keeping you from experiencing the joy of being fully known, the assurance of being happy with who you are where you are, and the contentment that accompanies a life completely surrendered to His single purpose for you.

Make yourself a cup of coffee or tea, find your Bible and bring a receiving heart to your favorite place of fellowship. Now get ready for some life-changing thoughts to ponder and introspective questions to answer as we stroll down the straight and narrow path of His single purpose for you.

H. NORMAN WRIGHT

1

Patterns for Problem Solving

*I know how to get along with humble means, and I
also know how to live in prosperity; in any and every
circumstance I have learned the secret of being filled and
going hungry, both of having abundance and suffering need. I
can do all things through Him who strengthens me.*

—PHILIPPIANS 4:12,13

Problems! Problems! Problems! Problems are a part of life. They can be
related not only to the one you live *without*, but also the one you live
with; not only *where* you live, but also *how* you live; not just *where* you
work, but also with *whom* you work; not only *how* much money you
have, but also *what* you believe about the money you don't have. The list
goes on and on.

James 1 says that you *will* have problems. But you can choose your
responses to them. You can either view them as opportunities for
growth—profit, or as excuses for failure—loss. How you see your problems will determine whether they become building blocks or stumbling
blocks. Consider the following five possibilities and reflect upon ways
you are responding to your problems:

- *Curse the problem.* This, in essence, means adding a negative
  opinion to the negative facts of the situation—in other words,
  compounding the negativity.
- *Nurse the problem.* Choosing to focus time and attention on
  the problem itself rather than on its solution.
- *Rehearse the problem.* Replaying the problem until you are
  actually thinking about little other than the problem.
- *Disperse the problem.* This is a technique used in tackling sci-
  entific problems. It requires breaking a problem down into its
  component parts; then working through each part until an
  answer is reached. As the component problems are solved, the
  big problem is also solved. This principle is effective for all of
  life. Overwhelming problems can be solved when the smaller

issues of the whole are dealt with one issue at a time.

- *Reverse the problem.* Seek out the positive. No situation or circumstance is 100 percent bad. Some glimmer of hope, some ray of light is tucked in every obstacle. Recognize negativity for what it is—a distraction from a positive solution. Dismiss the negativity. Of course, you should not ignore the problem in hopes that it will go away. To the contrary! You dispose of the negative by: facing the problem and facing your negative response to it; making a conscious decision that the negative response is going to do nothing to solve the problem; and in that light, refusing to dwell upon the negative by turning instead to the positive. Only you can reverse the way you *feel* about a problem.[1]

So...what pattern do you usually choose to solve problems? Let's look at what David did when he and his men were hiding from King Saul in a cave (see 1 Sam. 19—24). He had a mess of problems. The men who accompanied him were described as being "in distress, in debt and discontented." As David stood before them, they were probably surprised when he declared, "I will bless the Lord at all times; His praise shall continually be in my mouth" (Ps. 34:1, *Amp.*).

What a shock! Praise at a time of despair. Have you ever done that? Have you ever thanked God for your singleness when your heart was aching for a mate?

Praise at a time of loneliness or relational loss. Now, that takes faith! Praise when you're discontented. That will really turn your life around!

QUESTIONS FOR REFLECTION

Are you responding like David did in the cave?
Are you feeling threatened, forgotten or meaningless?
What is the glimmer of hope hidden in your cave?
What can you praise God for right now?
What new patterns will you choose for solving your problems?

Note

1. William Mitchell, *Winning in the Land of Giants* (Nashville: Thomas Nelson Publishers, 1995), pp. 27-28, adapted.

2

Lonely or Alone

[Lord] turn to me and be gracious to me,
for I am lonely and afflicted.
—PSALM 25:16 *(AMP.)*

What does it mean to be lonely? David cried out to God, "I cry," "I complain," "My spirit grows faint," "No one cares about me" (see Ps. 142:1-4, *NIV*).

As we hear in these words from David, loneliness is the feeling that you don't count, that you've been cut off from others, isolated, deserted or even banished from relationships with others. It's the feeling that even though you are in a room full of people, you are still all alone.

The word "lonely" has a mournful and eerie sound. It is cold like the earth in winter when the birds and flowers have abandoned it.

Singles commonly perceive loneliness as a sign of relational failure and inadequacy because people were created for relationship. Thus, singles sometimes feel ashamed when they are lonely. Why shame?

John Powell's book *Why Am I Afraid to Tell You Who I Am?*, provides the answer: If I tell you who I am, you might not like who I am, and that is all I have! Therefore we live with the fear of rejection in lonely castles we have erected with bricks of self-protection. Ask yourself the following questions:

Am I expecting other people to know that I am lonely? Am I expecting others to reach out to me? Am I expecting others to read my mind and know my situation? Am I afraid of letting others know me?

Sometimes the reason you feel lonely has to do with the kind of people you're drawn to. It could be you are in relationship with takers rather than givers. If so, it's time to reassess your choice of friends.

Also realize that no one person can meet all of your needs. Only Jesus knows the heart of each one of us. He is the only friend who will never leave or forsake you.

Jesus felt the pangs of loneliness. He was misunderstood by the masses and only partially understood by His disciples. He suffered loneliness in the garden of Gethsemane, in Pilate's judgment hall and upon the cross (see Matt. 26—27). His heart of love must have felt the full force of anguish that accompanies loneliness.

Jesus suffered loneliness that He might draw us into intimate relationship with Himself. For it is only when we take time to be *alone* with Him that we can know freedom from loneliness in its purest sense.

Are you lonely? Who knows about it? Perhaps this is the time to say, "I don't have to be lonely. I'm going to reach out to God and other people." Vulnerability requires risk. But Jesus risked everything for you so you might never face the loneliness of being all alone again. You can be joined to Him. Have you made that choice?

QUESTIONS FOR REFLECTION

God can use your loneliness to draw you into a deeper relationship with Himself. Take inventory of your prayer life. If you are especially lonely, ask yourself: Am I spending enough time alone with Him? Am I lonely because I would rather be alone than become vulnerable? What steps can I take to reach out to God and others?

3

How Can I Know God's Will?

Trust in the Lord with all your heart and lean
not on your own understanding.

—PROVERBS 3:5

Struggles with knowing God's will are not limited to big decisions; they are also a part of our everyday lives. We are daily confronted with questions such as, Where should I live? Is this the car I should buy? Which of these three job offers should I take? Is it God's will that I continue this relationship? What is His will for staying single or getting married?

But before these questions can be asked, you must first answer the question, Am I willing and ready to do God's will? Only if the answer is yes are you ready to ask the previous questions.

Keep in mind that His will may take you by surprise. This element of surprise is best expressed in Isaiah 55:8,9:

"For My thoughts are not your thoughts, neither are your ways My ways," declares the Lord. "For as the heavens are higher than the earth, so are My ways higher than your ways and My thoughts than your thoughts."

If you want to discover and do God's will, consider the following words.

The first word is *initiative.* Jesus showed our need for this in John 5:19: "I tell you the truth, the Son can do nothing by himself; he can do only what he sees his Father doing, because whatever the Father does the Son also does" *(NIV).*

Lloyd Ogilvie, the Chaplain of the United States Senate, has an interesting perspective:

Dr. James Dobson, in his helpful book *God's Will,* tells a penetrating story from Reverend Everett Howard, a veteran missionary to the Cape Verde Islands for 26 years. His call to the mission field has implications for all of us.

After finishing college and dental school, Howard was still uncertain about God's will for his life. One night he went into the sanctuary of the church where his father was serving as pastor. He knelt down at the altar and took a piece of paper on which he wrote all the things he was ready to do for God. He signed his name at the bottom and waited for some sign of God's affirmation and presence, but nothing happened. He took his paper again, thinking he might have left something out—still no response from the Lord. He waited and waited. Then it happened. He felt the Lord speaking within him. The Lord told him to tear up the sheet.

You're going about it all wrong, He said gently. *Son, I want you to take a blank piece of paper and sign it on the bottom, and let Me fill it in.*

Howard responded, and God guided a spectacular missionary career from that day forward.

God is not as interested in our commitment to what we decide to do for Him as He is in what we will allow Him to do through us. Our task is not to list the accomplishments of our plans for service, but to give Him a blank sheet and let Him fill it in.[1]

Let God take the *initiative*; then join Him in the walk. The closer you are to Jesus, the easier it will be to understand this act of obedience. Agree to partner with Him in every decision.

The second word is *timing.* "There is an appointed time for everything. And there is a time for every event under heaven" (Eccles. 3:1). God's timing is perfect. He is never too early or too late. Waiting may be the best step you can take until all indicators say, "Yes, this is the time to take action; yes, this is the mate for you; yes, this is the way, walk in it."

The last word may be difficult. It's *submit.* As the verse for today indicates, if you want to know and do God's will there can't be a power struggle between you and God. The more you value control and power, the greater the struggle you will have. But along with God's will being dependent upon His initiative and His timing, He must also be in charge.[2]

QUESTIONS FOR REFLECTION

In what ways have you allowed God to take the initiative in your life as a single? Are you really trusting His timing? Are you daily submitting to His lordship? How does your life show that you are leaning upon His understanding?

Notes

1. Lloyd S. Ogilvie, *Silent Strength for My Life* (Eugene, Oreg.: Harvest House, 1990), p. 308.

2. Ronny S. Floyd, *Choices* (Nashville, Tenn.: Broadman & Holman, 1994), pp. 112-114, adapted, and H. Norman Wright, *With All My Strength* (Ann Arbor, Mich.: Servant Publications, 1996), December 14.

4

How Can I Change?

The word of God is living and active. Sharper than any
double-edged sword, it penetrates even to dividing soul
and spirit, joints and marrow; it judges the thoughts
and attitudes of the heart.
—HEBREWS 4:12 *(NIV)*

"I can't change. I've tried and tried. It's impossible. I'm stuck." Many people actually believe these words. They are frustrated with their efforts. They try to break negative habits, such as blowing up or spending too much money, but they can't seem to change. Yet God's Word says emphatically that we *can* change.

A great story about change, or the lack of it, is told by Tim Hansel about a man who attended his 40-year high school reunion.

His friend left with excitement about all the changes and accomplishments his former classmates would report. This is what Tim wrote:

> I said, "Well, how was the reunion?"
>
> "Tim," the man said, "it was one of the saddest experiences of my life."
>
> "Good grief," I said, more than a little surprised. "What happened?"
>
> "It wasn't what happened, but what didn't happen. It has been 40 years, 40 years—and they haven't changed. They had simply gained weight, changed clothes, gotten jobs...but they hadn't really changed. And what I experienced was maybe one of the most tragic things I could ever imagine about life. For reasons I can't fully understand, it seems as though some people choose not to change."[1]

Change *is* possible for those of us who are believers in Christ Jesus because our faith is an inward transformation, not just an outward conformity. When Paul says, "My little children, of whom I travail in birth again until *Christ be formed in you*" (Gal. 4:19, *KJV*, italics added), he is telling us that we have to let Jesus live *in* and *through* us.

In Ephesians 4:23,24 we are told to "be renewed in the spirit of your mind...put on the new man, which after God is created in righteousness and true holiness" *(KJV)*. The "new man" has to be put on from the inside. We are able to put on the new man because God has placed Jesus Christ within us. We are to let Him work *within us*. Get it? From the inside out! That means we must give Him access to our memory banks where past experiences that need to be relinquished are stored.

Look again at Hebrews 4:12. The word "active" actually means "energize." God's Word energizes us for change. How? The apostle Paul says, "We demolish arguments and every pretension that sets itself up against the knowledge of God, and we take captive every thought to make it obedient to Christ" (2 Cor. 10:5, *NIV*).

As a child perhaps you played a game called "Capture the Flag." As adults we need to engage in capturing our thoughts. Why? Because negative feelings and relationship problems usually start there.

But how can we capture our thoughts? One way is by memorizing Scripture.

Can you think of some thoughts you would like to be rid of today? Ask God to make you aware of those thoughts as soon as they pop into your mind. Put them in writing. Then write the thoughts you would like to use to replace them. Read the new thoughts aloud several times a day.

QUESTIONS FOR REFLECTION

What habits do you need to change?
What negative thought patterns will you begin to replace today?
What are some of the positive thoughts you would like to incorporate into your thought life beginning today?

Note
1. Tim Hansel, *Holy Sweat* (Waco, Tex.: Word Books, 1987), p. 55.

5

My Enemy, the Calendar

Come to me, all you who are weary and burdened, and I will
give you rest. Take my yoke upon you and learn from me, for
I am gentle and humble in heart, and you will find rest for
your souls. For my yoke is easy and my burden is light.
—MATTHEW 11:28-30 *(NIV)*

Look at your calendar. Go ahead, take it out and look at it. What is it saying to you? Is every hour packed with activity? Some calendars are like that day after day, week after week.

Many singles would like a calendar with 60-day months and 48-hour days because they're trying to cram too much into their lives. Unfortunately, their new calendars would soon be overfilled, too. The difficulty is not the calendar; it's who is in charge of the calendar.

Because you're single, it is common to think you either have more time than you do or want to fill every minute so you don't have to feel the pangs of loneliness that singleness can bring.

Can you identify with the hectic lifestyle described by the following poem?

> This is the age
> Of the half-read page
> and the mad dash
> With the nerves tight
> The plane hop
> With the brief stop
> The lamp tan
> In a short span
> The Big Shot
> In a good spot
> And the brain strain
> And the heart pain
> And the cat naps
> Till the spring snaps
> And the fun's done.

No, this poem was not just written to describe our time. It was written in 1949 and appeared in the *Saturday Evening Post*. If the author, Virginia Brasier, were still writing, I wonder what words she would use to reflect our modern lifestyles.

Your calendar need not be an enemy. Instead, see it as a servant to be managed.

We all need a time of rest—a time of uninterrupted quiet solitude when we can recharge. But for many, making time for rest is an uphill battle. Some think rest is unnecessary, a waste, undeserved and a by-product of laziness. Dr. Richard Foster described his own battle for rest:

> After a certain amount of immersion in public life, I begin to burn out. And I have noticed that I burn out inwardly long before I do outwardly. Hence, I must be careful not to become a frantic bundle of hollow energy, busy among people but devoid of life. I must learn when to retreat, like Jesus, and experience the recreating power of God....And along our journey we need to discover numerous "tarrying places" where we can receive "heavenly manna."[1]

QUESTIONS FOR REFLECTION

So...Who's in charge of your life? Is it the calendar or you?
Either choice isn't the best. You have one other...it's God.

Note
1. H. Norman Wright, *With All My Strength* (Ann Arbor, Mich.: Servant Publications, 1996), adapted from December devotion.

6

The High Cost
of Anger

*He who is slow to anger is better than the mighty, he who
rules his [own] spirit than he who takes a city.*
—PROVERBS 16:32 *(AMP.)*

"I get so angry. I'm tired of being single. Even the Church treats me like
a second-class citizen. And to top it off...."

The list went on as this individual talked about her anger. Perhaps you
can identify with being angry. Most of us can. It happens. Some become
consumed by it. Their lives are driven by anger toward everyone and
everything. But they don't understand the nature of anger.

A few years ago a book titled *Anger Kills* was published. A strong title,
describing an absolute truth. Anger when out of control can kill you.
This emotion prepares your body for action. Did you know that when
you are angry your blood clots much more quickly, additional adrenaline
is released into your bloodstream and your muscles tense up? Your blood
pressure increases from 130 to 230, and your heart beats faster—often up
to 220 beats per minute or higher. People have had strokes and heart
attacks during fits of anger because of the increased blood pressure.

When your anger is not released, your body remains ready for action.
Your heart continues to beat rapidly, blood pressure continues to rise
and blood chemicals fluctuate. The results can harm you physically.
These are only the physical symptoms of anger.

Undealt with anger also has emotional and spiritual consequences.
Anger unreleased turns into resentment—the desire for revenge. But the
anger hurts the one who carries it far more than the one who is the
object of it.

Dr. S. I. McMillen's book *None of These Diseases* tells the story of a
visit Dale Carnegie made to Yellowstone National Park. Observing the
grizzly bears feeding, a guide told Carnegie that the grizzly bear could
whip any animal in the West with the exception of the buffalo and the
Kodiak bear.

That very night as people sat watching a grizzly eat, they noticed the
grizzly would allow only one animal to eat with him—a skunk. Now the

grizzly could have beaten the skunk in any fight. He probably resented the skunk and wanted to get even with it for coming into his own feeding domain. But he didn't attack the skunk. Why? Because he knew the high cost of getting even! It wouldn't be worth it. Perhaps that's why Ephesians 4:26 says, "Do not let the sun go down on your anger [resentment or bitterness]."

Let's look at the result of anger in the life of Nabal (see 1 Sam. 25). David sent some of his men to Nabal, a very wealthy man. They wanted some food, but instead Nabal gave them a rebuke and sent them away. Upon hearing this, David gathered his men together and set out to fight Nabal. But Abigail, Nabal's wife, heard what her husband had done. So she gathered a large store of food, went out to meet them, and appeased David and his men with her gift.

> And Abigail came to Nabal, and behold, he was holding a feast in his house like the feast of a king. And his heart was merry, for he was very drunk; so she told him nothing at all until the morning light. But in the morning, when the wine was gone out of Nabal, and his wife told him these things, his heart died within him, and he became [paralyzed, helpless as] a stone. And about ten days after that, the Lord smote Nabal and he died (1 Sam. 25:36-38, *Amp.*).

The phrase, his heart died within him, in the original could mean he had a stroke or a heart attack. Why did this happen? Nabal probably reacted to his wife's actions with intense anger.

Think about that the next time you are angry!

QUESTIONS FOR REFLECTION

Are you angry about the load you are carrying as a single person?
In what other areas of your life are you harboring anger?
What steps can you take to eliminate your hurts and anger?
Have you considered the high cost of your anger?

7

Reversing Rejection

[So that we might be] to the praise and the commendation of
His glorious grace favor and mercy, which He so freely
bestowed on us in the Beloved.

—EPHESIANS 1:6 *(AMP.)*

Outlaws were common in the Old West. You've seen them in Western movies. Often they wore black hats and rode black horses. They were many times seen riding away from bounty hunters and were unaccepted by communities they visited. They learned to live with the isolation usually brought about by rejection. Nobody wanted them...except for the purpose of reward—dead or alive.

Many singles today feel just like outlaws. Are you one of them? If so, you probably don't feel wanted by another significant person or a significant employer or a singles group or even the Church. You feel cut off, isolated and often lonely. Sometimes you feel disconnected, like an island with no landmass to connect you to the mainland. You may not have a bounty hunter pursuing you, but wish you did. Do you sometimes feel that anyone would be better than no one?

Rejection is the pits. It hurts. As someone said, "It stinks, and the odor is so bad, you can't even identify it!" If you are feeling rejection, you probably feel unworthy of a relationship. And the more rejection you have experienced, the more sensitive you become to actual or even imagined slights by others.

Rejection can become a vicious cycle: You expect it to happen; and the more it does happen, the more you tend to reject yourself. Therefore, you begin to make discouraging remarks to yourself that impact your relationships with the significant people around you. Your needs for acceptance and approval place a burden on them to give and give and give to you. And when they don't (or can't), guess how you feel? That's right...rejected! The never-ending vicious cycle then repeats itself.

So, what can you do? The first step is to discover how you reject yourself. Listen to what you say to yourself about yourself. If you're making negative, self-rejecting statements, begin to challenge them.

Focus on the way God sees and accepts you. He sees you as worth the precious blood of Jesus:

Knowing that you were not redeemed with perishable things like silver or gold from your futile way of life inherited from your forefathers, but with precious blood, as of a lamb unblemished and spotless, the blood of Christ (1 Pet. 1:18,19).

Read the following statement each day for a week and you will soon see a difference.

This then, is the wonder of the Christian message; that God is a kind God who loves me with a love that is not turned off by my sins, my failures, my inadequacies, my insignificance. I am not a stranger in a terrifying universe. I am not an anomalous disease crawling upon the face of an insignificant speck in the vast emptiness of space. I am not a nameless insect waiting to be crushed by an impersonal boot. I am not a miserable offender cowering under the glare of an angry deity.

I am a man beloved by God Himself. I have touched the very heart of the universe, and have found His name to be love. And that love has reached me, not because I have merited God's favor—not because I have anything to boast about, but because of who He is, and because of what Christ has done for me in the Father's name. And I can believe this about God (and therefore about myself), because Christ has come from the Father and has revealed by His teaching, by His life, by His death, by His very person that this is what God is like: He is "full of grace."[1]

It's true, people will reject us. But our hope and comfort come from knowing that God never does.

QUESTIONS FOR REFLECTION

Are you caught in the cycle of rejection?
What negative statements have you been making about yourself?
When will you take the necessary steps to reverse the cycle in your life?

Note
1. Joseph R. Cooke, *Free for the Taking* (Grand Rapids, Mich.: Fleming H. Revell, 1975), p. 29.

8

Laughter: The Gift That Cures

A glad heart makes a cheerful countenance, but by sorrow of heart the spirit is broken....All the days of the desponding and afflicted are made evil [by anxious thoughts and forebodings], but he who has a glad heart has a continual feast [regardless of circumstances].
—PROVERBS 15:13-15 (AMP.)

Laughter, it makes the world go around.

Someone said:

Laugh a little. No, laugh a lot.

These are words of wisdom. Laughter is one of God's gifts. Life is filled with incidents that lend themselves to not just a snicker, but an uncontrolled siege of laughter. Are you known as a person who can laugh? One who enjoys life? What's the laughter level in your world? Do you laugh a little or a lot?

It could be that what you don't have is eluding you because you are refusing to take God's antidote for unhappiness. Solomon tells us that God intended laughter to be our medicine during times of physical, emotional and spiritual brokenness: "A joyful heart is good medicine, but a broken spirit dries up the bones" (Prov. 17:22).

Humor relaxes. It relieves tension. It brings a sense of balance into life. It provides a respite from the heaviness of life's concerns and griefs. Those who don't laugh tend to shrivel up like dried-out prunes.

Yes, it's true that times will occur when the seriousness of life makes it difficult to laugh. But generally, we have a choice.

Laughter can also involve our moral choices. We do have to avoid compromising our Christian standards; but for the most part, laugher enriches our lives.

Remember Lazarus in John 11, the man whom Jesus brought back to life? Have you ever related his story to laughter?

Judson Edwards wrote a fascinating statement about the play, *Laughing with Lazarus.* Consider his words:

Eugene O'Neill's play *Laughing with Lazarus* begins with Jesus' raising of Lazarus from the dead and deals with the change this miracle makes in Lazarus' life. After he has been raised, Lazarus becomes fearless. Try as they might, the Jewish leaders cannot stifle his gladness. Laughter is his trademark, and everywhere he goes people are warmed and enlivened by his presence. Because he has learned that even the Final Enemy cannot defeat him, Lazarus is eternally infected with joy. It's a scenario we uptight Christians would do well to consider.

Sheer fiction you say? A figment of the playwright's imagination? Not really—most of us are like Lazarus! We are the people who have been raised to walk in newness of life. WE are the ones who insist that the hope of the resurrection affects us profoundly the moment we choose Jesus. Every last one of us who claims to be a Christian has an inheritance: the same joy Lazarus experienced after his miracle at Bethany; the same fearlessness; the same contagious freedom.

The only bucket of water hanging over the fire is our unbelief. Most of us are at heart unbelievers. We refuse to accept all of the incredible implications of calvary. We believe the lie that God is not for us. Though the prison door stands wide open, we huddle in self-imposed chains and refuse to claim our liberty. Unlike Lazarus, we refuse to leave the tomb. We cannot convince our hearts to believe that laughter is our birthright.

But, thank God, it is never too late! The door stands eternally open. And our joy and peace are sure indicators that we have walked through it.

So, do you want to know just how Christian you really are? Then don't listen to your creeds or your prayers. They come from your head and reflect your mind. Listen, instead, to your laughter. It comes from your soul and reflects your heart. Your laughter will tell you unfailingly of your faith in God.[1]

QUESTIONS FOR REFLECTION

Are you willing to accept the gift that cures? Will you take God's prescription for your unhealthy attitudes? How much time do you spend laughing? What changes are you willing to make today to cultivate a sense of humor?

Note
1. Judson Edwards, *Regaining Control of Your Life* (Minneapolis: Bethany, 1989), pp. 47-48.

9

Marriage: Is It for Me?

But each has his own special gift from God,
one of this kind and one of another.
—1 CORINTHIANS 7:7 *(AMP.)*

All right, let's talk marriage. Some singles want to be married; some don't.

Unfortunately, those who are already married (even those in the Church) just assume that anyone who is single desperately wants to be married. Look at the majority of books in the singles' section of any Christian bookstore. Most of these books cover topics such as dating, how to find the best mate or how to avoid the duds!

Remaining single is not necessarily a negative. Not everyone is called to be married. Have you ever given thought to a *chosen* single lifestyle? Singleness can be a gift.

Consider what Tim Stafford has said about singleness:

God may want you to be single. He wants everyone to be single for at least a part of life. And the Bible doesn't talk about singleness as being second rate. In fact, the Bible speaks positively about it.

In the Middle Ages, Christians went too far, and *marriage* was regarded as second rate. In recent times, we seem to have swung the other way. Balance is the key. Both marriage and singleness are gifts from God.

Ponder for a moment the following facts about our Lord: Jesus Christ never married. He never had sexual intercourse. Yet He was perfect, and perfectly fulfilled. He lived the kind of life we want to imitate. That doesn't mean we should all want to be single; undoubtedly marriage is the best way for most men and women. But singleness need not be unhappy.

Paul wasn't married either, at least at the height of his career. He addressed the single life in 1 Corinthians 7, calling it a gift. (Strange that this is the one gift most would prefer to exchange.) And Jesus Himself, in Matthew 19:10-12, talks positively about the reasons some people should remain unmarried....

It saddens me to see single people who live life as though waiting for something or someone to happen to them. They act as though they are in limbo, waiting to become capable of life when that magic day at the altar finally arrives.

Of course, singles who live in this constant state of disappointment often become such poor specimens of humanity that no one wants to marry them. More often they do get married only to discover that they haven't received the key to life: the initiative and character they should have developed before marriage is exactly what they need in marriage. And they are still lonely and frustrated....

Our culture, especially our Christian culture, has stressed repeatedly that a good marriage takes work. It holds up for admiration those who have formed "a good marriage." But I've seldom heard anyone emphasize the fact that a good single life also takes work. I've never heard anyone compliment a person for having created a good single lifestyle. This creates an atmosphere in which telling single people they have received a gift is rather like convincing a small child that liver ought to taste good because it's "good for you."

Singleness, as I see it, is not so much a state we've arrived at as an open door, a set of opportunities for us to follow up.[1]

So, if you believe singleness might be your calling, try it for a specific period of time. Eliminate dating for six months or a year. If you find your heart's desire is unmet, that's all right. Discovering your gift may require some experimentation. It's better to test it than to spend your life wondering.

QUESTIONS FOR REFLECTION

Do you want to get married because you feel pressured by others, or is marriage something you feel called to? If God asked you to stay single for greater power in ministry, would you say yes to Him? Are you willing to surrender this area of your life to Him?

Note
1. Tim Stafford, *A Love Story* (Grand Rapids, Mich.: Zondervan Publishing, 1977), pp. 91-93.

10

You and Your Money

Owe nothing to anyone except to love one another; for he who loves his neighbor has fulfilled the law.
—ROMANS 13:8

You're at a restaurant with friends. The loan officer of your bank walks by, says hello and suggests you pay him a visit to discuss some "concerns."

Do you feel discomfort, guilt, anxiety...? The amount of tension that can arise when we are in the presence of a person to whom we owe money can be quite stressful.

How *are* you and your bank getting along?

We either view the bank as a friend or a source of anxiety. It's true, we all need money and there never seems to be enough. Prices climb, the paycheck shrinks, an unexpected bill comes in, a check bounces and the car won't start. We find ourselves spending more than we're making. Sound familiar?

Some people, however, have a different problem with money—they love it:

For the *love* of money is a root of all sorts of evil, and some by longing for it have wandered away from the faith, and pierced themselves with many a pang (1 Tim. 6:10, italics added).

Money becomes their reason for existence, their source of ambition, their goal in life. In other words, it's their god. And singles are not exempt from this form of idolatry. Often they face an even greater struggle than marrieds because they don't have to spend it on anyone else!

What part does money play in your life? Think about these questions:

- What percentage of the day do you spend worrying about money?
- Do you spend more time thinking or worrying about money than you spend praying each day?
- When you're feeling down, discouraged or hurt, do you jump into the car and go on a shopping spree to make yourself feel better? (You may not want to answer that one.)

- Does your self-worth fluctuate according to your net worth?
- To what extent is money the source of arguments between you and others, such as family members?
- If you listed all of your canceled checks or charges, what message would they tell about the place money has in your life?
- To what extent do you operate on a well-defined budget?
- Do you have a plan to handle unexpected extra money you might receive? (That does happen, you know.)
- Do you pray about the money God entrusts to you, asking Him how to use it for His kingdom and glory?
- How much of the money you have spent is earned rather than borrowed?

One of the greatest sources of tension happens when money is loaned to family members or close friends. For example, you borrow money to pay off a school loan, but instead spend it for a great deal on a new computer or vehicle you just have to have. How would they handle the switch in plans? How would you feel if someone did that to you?

Remember:

- Friendships have been lost over loaning money.
- Families have been torn apart over loaning money.
- Bankruptcies have occurred over borrowing funds.

Keep in mind that when you owe on your credit cards, you become a servant to the one you owe. Proverbs admonishes: "The rich rule over the poor, and the borrower is servant to the lender" (22:7, *NIV*).

When you are tempted to borrow, to charge it and to explain how desperately you need this item—wait. Delay, pray and look away! Consider your current bills. It may take longer to obtain some things, but you'll have a greater sense of freedom in the long run.[1]

QUESTIONS FOR REFLECTION

Is your bank a friend or a source of anxiety?
Are you a servant to the lender? What is the total of your debt?
What steps are you willing to take to reduce your deficit spending?

Note
1. Lloyd John Ogilvie, *Silent Strength for My Life* (Eugene, Oreg.: Harvest House Publishers, 1990), p. 321, adapted.

11

Lust or Love

I made a covenant with my eyes
not to look lustfully at a girl.
—JOB 31:1 *(NIV)*

Lust—God included this topic in His Word because He knew that each of us would encounter a struggle with it at times.

Most men and women don't know what God's Word says about this subject. So let's look at Scripture to see what He has to say about it. What does the word "lust" mean? Four Hebrew and three Greek words can be translated into the English word "lust" or "to lust after." In this devotion we will explore two of these words.

The first is found in Exodus 15. Moses and the people of Israel sang a song of praise to God after their deliverance from Egypt. In verse 9 they sang: "The enemy said, 'I will pursue, I will overtake;... My *desire* shall be gratified against them; I will draw out my sword, my hand shall destroy them.'" The word "desire" in the *New American Standard Bible* is translated "lust" in other versions.

The second word we will explore is "hedonism." This is an English word derived from the Greek word *hedone*, translated "lust" in James 4 verses 1 and 3 in the *King James Version*. Each Scripture where the word *hedone* is used, whether translated "lust" or "pleasure," puts the emphasis on gratification of natural or sinful desires. You've probably read this word in literature. Some people openly refer to themselves as hedonists. You may even know some!

God designed sex to be the physical part of a marital relationship where oneness and intimacy are given full expression. Within God's design, desire—even strong desire—is not wrong; it is good.

The Greek word *epithumia* illustrates this. It denotes strong desire of any kind. And because marriage is God's design, strong desire within marriage is not only natural, it is also blessed. Even the anticipatory desire that precedes marriage is natural and blessed.

But lust becomes a problem when people treat each other as objects to gratify their own selfishness. When sex is misused in a lustful, selfish and dishonoring way, it becomes a weapon that wounds rather than a tool that creates the fulfillment of a loving union.

So what, then, is lust?

Noticing that a person is sexually attractive is not lust. Lust is born when we turn a simple awareness into a preoccupying fantasy.

When we invite sexual thoughts to lodge in our minds and nurture them, we pass from simple awareness into lust. Luther put it this way: "We cannot help it if birds fly over our heads. It is another thing if we invite them to build nests in our hair.[1]

Lewis Smedes describes lust this way:

It is foolish to identify every erotic feeling with lust. There is a sexual desire that feels like a lonely vacuum yearning to be filled, a longing for intimacy that broods unsettled in one's system. To identify this as lust is to brand every normal sexual need as adultery. Eros, the longing for personal fulfillment, must not be confused with lust, the untamed desire for another's body. Nor is every feeling of attraction toward an exciting person the spark of lust....But attraction can become captivity; and when we have become captives of the thought, we have begun to lust. When the sense of excitement conceives a plan to use a person, when attraction turns into a scheme, we have crossed beyond erotic excitement into spiritual adultery. There need be no guilt when we have a sense of excitement and tension in the presence of a sexually stimulating person; but we also need to be alert to where that excitement can lead.[2]

It is possible to lead a lust-free life. Prayerfully ask God for the assistance you need. Then take responsibility for your thought life. Starve lustful thoughts. Fill your mind with Scripture. Feed on those thoughts that will glorify Him. You cannot think about lust and the Lord at the same time. You can choose to meditate on those things that dishonor God and others, or you can choose to meditate on His love and those things that bring honor to him. Lust or love—it's a matter of choice.

QUESTIONS FOR REFLECTION

Can you identify the differences between lust and love?
If you are struggling with lust, are you willing to take responsibility for your thought life? How much time have you spent memorizing God's Word? Will you make the choice to start today?

Notes

1. R. C. Sproul, *Pleasing God* (Wheaton, Ill.: Tyndale, 1988), p. 79, adapted.
2. Lewis Smedes, *Sex for Christians* (Grand Rapids: William D. Eardmans, 1976), p. 210.

12

Self-Control

Add to your faith virtue, to virtue knowledge,
to knowledge self-control, to self-control perseverance,
to perseverance godliness.
—2 PETER 1:5,6 *(NKJV)*

Lust is an issue we all struggle with in one way or another. We've talked about it and defined it as it applies to sex. Paul is saying that training ourselves to be godly (see 1 Tim. 4:7) covers other parts of our lives as well.

In 1 Thessalonians 4:4-6 *(NIV)*, Paul says, "Each of you should learn to control his own body in a way that is holy and honorable, not in passionate lust like the heathen, who do not know God; and that in this matter no one should wrong his brother or take advantage of him. The Lord will punish men for all such sins, as we have already told you and warned you."

That's strong language, but it's important to follow. As Christians, we're called to be different from other people. We are to surrender the contol of our lives in every area including sex, anger, thoughts, money, food, power, alcohol, friendship and relational boundaries. Let's look at some of the steps we can take to live more fully surrendered Christian lives:

- Be accountable to a small group or another person that you can be honest with and know will support you. Not only will this person or group pray for you, but they will also ask you direct questions about how you're doing as well.
- Pray specifically for your own purity in thought and action.
- Memorize the Word of God. "I have hidden your word in my heart that I might not sin against you" (Ps. 119:11, *NIV*). Memorize that passage today! Ask God for His strength "that He would grant you, according to the riches of His glory through His Spirit in the inner man; so that Christ may dwell in your hearts through faith; and that you, being rooted and grounded in love, may be able to comprehend with all the saints what is the breadth and length and height and depth, and to know the love of Christ which surpasses knowledge, that you may be filled up to all the fullness of God" (Eph. 3:16-19).

- Watch your thought life and your eyes! What we think about and focus our eyes on can fan that spark of lust into a raging fire. Avoid sexually tempting situations—you know what they are for you. It could include TV programs, R-rated movies, magazines, interests or clubs with sexually explicit entertainment.

Because sexual temptations can be the most consuming for singles, it is important to remember the counsel of Job who said, "I made a covenant with my eyes not to look lustfully at a girl!" (Job 31:1, *NIV*). It could mean avoiding that second look or keeping your eyes at eye level. It can also refer to what you do in your mind with that look. If you don't watch what you watch, you will get burned: "Can a man scoop fire into his lap without his clothes being burned?" (Prov. 6:27).

A minister once said: "One look of recognition, one look of appreciation, and no more looks!"

Holiness—it takes on a whole new meaning when we apply it to everyday struggles with sex, doesn't it? But it is possible.[1]

QUESTIONS FOR REFLECTION

Where do you need to gain greater self-control? Are you meeting with someone who is asking you the hard questions about the purity of your Christian life? Is your heart crying out for His power as you face daily temptations, or are you trying to handle your temptations alone? Do you desire to live a life of obedience to God today? If so, how much of His Word have you memorized? Are you struggling with sexual temptations? Have you made a covenant with your eyes?

Note
1. R. Kent Hughes, *Disciplines of a Godly Man* (Wheaton, Ill.: Crossway, 1991), pp. 29-31, adapted.

Listening Builds Relationships

Be quick to hear [a ready listener].
—JAMES 1:19 *(AMP.)*

One of the greatest gifts you can give to another person is the gift of listening. As James 1:19 tells us, we are to be ready listeners.

The Amplified Bible sheds light on the fact that listening is a gift you must be *quick* and *ready* to give.

It is a gift of such spiritual significance to others that it can recreate a sense of importance, hope and love where rejection, hopelessness and despair have previously wreaked havoc.

Proverbs 20:12 says, "The hearing ear and the seeing eye, the Lord has made both of them" *(Amp.)*. Listening is a tool God has provided for His creation to nurture and validate each other. But as with all other tools, you must learn how to use it.

Listening requires that you make a full investment of your spiritual, emotional and physical senses. It requires you to see with the eyes of your heart. Listening is looking beyond the spoken words and seeing what the person's actions are saying as well. To really listen you must be willing to focus fully on the other person.

Listening requires using the ears of your heart; hearing not just the spoken words, but the unspoken words of the spirit that are too painful to share. It may mean leaning your spiritual ear against the emotional chest of another to hear the heartbeat of one who is under attack.

Listening requires an openness to whatever is being shared: feelings, attitudes or concerns. This can be difficult because real listening means that you give up not only the desire to fix it, but also to defend yourself. Defensiveness and listening are incompatible. Listening is putting yourself in a position to feel from the other person's point of view and to lovingly respond to whatever is being shared with you. You will often have to be silent when you would rather speak:

He who answers a matter before he hears the facts—it is folly and shame to him (Prov. 18:13, *Amp.*).

When you are listening, you are also receiving a gift. You are receiving an invitation to be a guest in the heart of another. Thoughtful guests are often welcomed to return because they have earned trust. And trust is the soil in which safe relationships are cultivated.

You can help others to deepen their roots in your friendship by setting an example. Take the initiative to share openly and lovingly. Respond with trust and gratitude. Welcome others into your life and you will find that others can make room for you too.

Keep in mind that men and women listen differently. Women tend to give more feedback to indicate they are tracking with the other person. Men tend to give less verbal feedback; and when they do, it means they agree with you. Thus, if you are a single woman, do not mistake a man's silence for being unheard. And if you are a single man, you can learn to be more open. (My book *What Men Want* will provide an in-depth look at the ways men listen.)

Remember, there is a distinct difference between listening and hearing. The goal of hearing is to gain content or information for your own purposes. In hearing, you are concerned about what is going on inside of *you* during the conversation. You are tuned in to your own responses, thoughts and feelings.

The goal of friendship, however, is to be a listener. If you want to be known as a friendly person, you will want to care for and empathize with others. The world needs those who listen because few people do. Years ago a man said, "Listen to all the conversations of the world between nations as well as married people. They are for the most part dialogues of the deaf." Sobering thought!

QUESTIONS FOR REFLECTION

Who do you really listen to in your life? Who needs your listening ear? What steps do you need to take to be a better listener?

14

Why, God, Why?

*"For I know the plans I have for you," declares the Lord,
"plans to prosper you and not to harm you, plans to
give you hope and a future."*
—JEREMIAH 29:11 *(NIV)*

"Bad hair" days, "fur-ball" days! No matter what you call them—some days don't feel worth living. Whether you're facing a morning of cold water and slippery soap in the shower or a life-changing day when a major calamity crumbles your hopes and crushes your heart, three questions usually arise:

- Why, God, why?
- When, God, when?
- Will I survive, God, will I really survive?

You wonder: *Why? Why me? Why now? Why this? Why, God, why?* If you are facing these questions, you're not alone. They are as old as humanity itself. Since the Fall, people have been trying to reconcile the basic goodness of God with the suffering of humanity. Only your belief about life will determine how you respond to your crisis.

Dr. Lloyd Ogilvie suggests the following:

First, we believe that problems including crisis, losses and anything that doesn't go our way is bad for us. Whatever disrupts the flow of our lives and is unpleasant or causes distress can't in any way be beneficial for us. Problems are a bother, an invasion, a disruption and they have no real benefit.

We also believe in entitlement. We deserve to live problem-free lives, especially if we're faithful, diligent, hard working and planning ahead.

The third belief has to do with God. If we believe in Him, serve Him, follow His Word, He will (or ought to) make sure our lives run smoothly, without any difficulty. We believe God owes us clear sailing in life.[1]

Remember Job, the man who lost it all in just one day? Job experienced one devastating crisis after another. He must have felt like he had spun the wheel of misfortune and lost it all. Everything went: his family, friends, possessions, wealth, reputation and health. After several days of silence Job began asking the questions many of us ask when facing loss:

"Why didn't I die at birth?"

"Why can't I die now?"

"Why has God done this to me?" (Have you ever felt this way and wondered, *Where is God?*)

Sixteen times Job asked God, "Why?"

Sixteen times God responded with silence. How could a loving God respond to a broken heart with silence? Silence not only sounds like a strange response, but it almost sounds cruel.

However, if God had given Job the answer to this question immediately, would Job have accepted it? Would you? Or would you argue against His answer? The truth is that you probably would not have understood God's reasoning. God's silence gives you the opportunity to learn to live by faith. It increases your ability to trust Him, which ultimately causes you to walk in deeper friendship with Him.

God does not explain all suffering in the world or the meaning of each crisis that occurs.

Just as God has arranged the seasons to produce growth in nature, He has arranged the seasonal experiences of your life for growth in character and relationship with Him. Some days bring sunshine; some bring storms. Both are necessary.

Only God knows the amount of pressure you can handle. First Corinthians 10:13 says that He will "not let you be tempted beyond what you can bear" *(NIV)*. But He does allow you to be tempted, feel pain and experience suffering. No, He does not always give you what you think you need, but He does give you what you need to produce growth.

When your question changes from Why? to What can I learn through this? then you will have the answer.[2]

QUESTIONS FOR REFLECTION

Are you feeling overwhelmed and deserted by the problems you are facing in your singleness today? Will you trust God even when He is silent? What lessons have you learned from your past sorrows? Are you willing to allow God to help you grow you through the problems of today?

Notes

1. Dr. Lloyd J. Ogilvie, *If God Cares Why Do I Still Have Problems?* (Waco, Tex.: Word Publishing, 1985), p. 18.
2. H. Norman Wright, *With All My Strength* (Ann Arbor, Mich.: Servant Publications, 1996), October 28, adapted.

15

Change? Never!

For I am the Lord, I do not change.
—MALACHI 3:6 *(NKJV)*

I resist change, what about you? It's okay to admit this. You and I get comfortable with our routines. It's not that we can't change; it's just that we'd rather not. Not all change is bad. We just don't want to move out of our comfort zones to experience it.

The twentieth century is resulting in more rapid changes than you or I can keep pace with. Just about the time you get used to your new computer and printer, it's out of date. By the time you finished paying for your new wardrobe, the latest styles are introduced, causing you to look five years behind the times. They even messed with the taste of Coke in the '80s. Now that's an outrage!

But let's think about change for a minute. In what ways are you different today from five years ago (aside from the obvious—age!)? Hopefully your changes throughout the past five years have brought improvement to the quality of your character.

Now, let's consider change as it relates to God. Or maybe you've never pondered His changelessness. Imagine this: You're at work, someone walks into the office and makes the following statement:

> Let me tell you something about God that you may already know or perhaps you don't know. God doesn't ever learn a thing. He knows all things. He doesn't have to go around spying on people to discover what's going on; He knows. Remember when you were in school and struggled in some class trying to learn something? Well, God cannot learn and has never learned. He doesn't need to. He knows everything instantly. He knows everything equally well. He never wonders about anything, never discovers anything, and is never amazed by anything. He also knows all the possibilities that can happen.[1]

The truth is that God doesn't change. Created things have a beginning and ending, but God doesn't. He has always been and always will be.

There was not a time when He did not exist. He does not grow older. He does not get wiser, stronger or weaker. He cannot change for the better. He is perfection. Scripture confirms this:

> They shall perish, but you go on forever. They will grow old, like worn-out clothing, and you will change them like a man putting on a new shirt and throwing away the old one! (Ps. 102:26, *TLB*).

> Listen to me, my people, my chosen ones! I alone am God. I am the First; I am the Last (Isa. 48:12, *TLB*).

God's *character* does not change. Because He *is* truth, His truth does not change. He does not have to take back anything He has ever said. Because He *is* mercy, His mercies toward you are new every morning. Because He *is* goodness, you can know that every good and perfect gift comes from Him. Because He is the promised lamb of God, you can trust in His promises and know that He will fulfill them concerning your life.

James speaks about God as one "with whom there is no variation or shadow due to change" (1:17, *RSV*). This verse refers to the fact that when a sundial is at high noon, it does not cast a shadow. God is always at high noon for you. You can depend upon Him. That's comforting.

God's *purposes* do not change. What God does in the context of time, He planned from eternity. All that He has committed Himself to do in His Word will be done.

It's difficult to comprehend everything about God with our finite minds and human thinking processes. But our inability to comprehend gives evidence to the vast difference between God and the people He created.[2]

QUESTIONS FOR REFLECTION

Where in your life are you afraid to face change? Will you make a decision today to trust God's unchangeable love to walk you through the hard places that confront you? What promises has He spoken into your heart that you need to trust Him for? What promises have you made to Him and to others that need to be fulfilled to reflect His life being lived through you?

Notes

1. A. W. Tozer, *The Knowledge of the Holy* (New York: Harper Brothers, 1961), pp. 61-62, adapted.
2. J. I. Packer, *Knowing God* (Downers Grove, Ill.: InterVarsity, 1973), pp. 68-73, adapted.

16

Worry: the Silent Killer

Do not be anxious about anything, but in everything,
by prayer and petition, with thanksgiving,
present your requests to God.
—PHILIPPIANS 4:6 *(NIV)*

You don't worry...do you? We all do at times. Unfortunately, some make worrying a lifestyle. Those who are married sometimes look at those who are single and wish they were there again—so much less to worry about—right? Wrong! Wrong! Whether married or single, situations occur that we can *choose* to worry about. The key word is "choose."

How would you define "worry"?

Originally the word meant "to kill a person or animal by compressing the throat; to strangle or choke" (see Matt. 13:22). Today, worry means "joy killer" or "to cause distress of mind; to make conscious and ill at ease."

Worry is fear. It is a result of the Fall. Worry is the silent, deadly killer of faith. It stalks and distorts one of God's invaluable gifts to us—our minds. Scripture has much to say about this brutal weapon used by our enemy to destroy our joy. Let's consider a few of these verses:

> I heard and my [whole inner self] trembled; my lips quivered at the sound. Rottenness enters into my bones and under me [down to my feet]; I tremble (Hab. 3:16, *Amp.*).

> Anxiety in a man's heart weighs it down (Prov. 12:25, *Amp.*).

> A tranquil mind gives life to the flesh (Prov. 14:30, *RSV*).

> All the days of the desponding and afflicted are made evil [by anxious thoughts and forebodings], but he who has a glad heart has a continual feast [regardless of circumstances] (Prov. 15:15, *Amp.*).

Worrying intensely about a threatening event will not prevent it from happening; instead it can actually help to bring the situation about!

Physicians report that EEG tests show brain wave differences in people who are worried.

Our thinking patterns affect how we perform. Proverbs says that "as he [or she] thinketh in his [or her] heart, so is he [or she]" (Prov. 23:7, KJV).

So...is it wrong to worry? Well, some say that worry accuses God of being a liar. These are strong words, but God *has* promised to meet our needs (see Phil. 4:19). Worry replies, "I don't think so." Worry also questions the sovereignty of God. In Romans 8:28 God promises to use everything that comes into our lives for good even though we don't understand why or how.

Worry can also be a sign that we feel abandoned by God. Yet Scripture says, "'I will never desert you, nor will I ever forsake you,' so that we confidently say, "'The Lord is my helper, I will not be afraid. What shall man do to me?'" (Heb. 13:5,6).

Worry is the chisel that chips away at the foundation of our faith. It causes us to believe the lie that our circumstances are greater than our God. But God has yet another promise: "Do not fear, for I am with you; do not be dismayed, for I am your God. I will strengthen you and help you; I will uphold you with my righteous right hand" (Isa. 41:10, *NIV*).

This scripture gives you confidence that:

1. You have nothing to fear. Why? Because I, God, am with you.
2. You should not be dismayed. Why? Because I am your God and I will *strengthen* you, *help* you and *uphold* you.

Did you know that *dismayed* is a word used to describe someone who looks around in bewilderment? Perhaps in the midst of your worry you're unsure of your direction and you feel helpless.

God promises to strengthen you. *Strengthen* means "to be alert or fortified." At the moment you need the direction, you will be alerted and fortified.

The word "help" in biblical Greek means "to surround." You will be protected on all sides. God will hedge you in with His protection.

Finally, "uphold" means "to sustain." That means He will keep you going when the going gets tough; He will make a way when there is no way; and when you feel like you just can't take one more step, He will carry you. So, with all that God has promised, why worry?

Reading and memorizing the promises in this devotional can counteract your tendency to worry. Begin each day by reading them aloud.

Allow the Holy Spirit to write them upon your heart. Then when you are tempted to worry, His Word will be there as a constant reminder of His faithfulness.[1]

What are the issues that have you worried today? What is your worry saying about your faith in God? Do you believe He is bigger than your circumstances? If so, how will you show Him that you believe in His faithfulness?

Note

1. H. Norman Wright, *With All My Strength* (Ann Arbor, Mich.: Servant Publications, 1996), August 31, adapted.

Guard Your Heart

*You will guard him and keep him in perfect and constant
peace whose mind [both its inclination and its character] is
stayed on You, because he commits himself to You, leans on
You, and hopes confidently in You.*

—ISAIAH 26:3 *(AMP.)*

Worry can make you feel like you can't see the forest for the trees. It can feel like you are being eaten alive.

Worry is best represented by the familiar scene at the Snake River in the Grand Teton National Park in Wyoming where colonies of beavers live along the riverbanks. Often you can see trees that are at various stages of being gnawed to the ground by the beavers. Some trees have slight rings around their trunks where these busy little animals have just begun to chew. Some manifest a barrenness where several inches of bark have been eaten away; others have already fallen to the ground because the beavers have gnawed through their trunks. Worry can have the same effect upon you. It can gradually eat away at your heart and mind until it has destroyed you!

God's Word paints the previous Snake River picture in Psalm 37:1-10. Notice how this Psalm begins: "Do not fret." The words are repeated again and again throughout this chapter. The dictionary defines "fret" as: "to eat away, gnaw, gall, vex, worry, agitate, wear away."

In addition to telling you not to fret, Psalm 37 gives positive substitutes for worry. First, it says, "Trust (lean on, rely on and be confident) in the Lord" (v. 3, *Amp.*). Trust is a matter of refusing to live an independent life or to cope with difficulties alone. It means going to a greater source for strength.

Second, verse four says, "Delight yourself also in the Lord" *(Amp.)*. To delight means to rejoice in God and what He has done for you. It helps to make a list of what He has done.

Verse five says, "Commit your way to the Lord" *(Amp.)*. Commitment is a definite act of the will; it involves releasing your worries and anxieties to Him.

This passage also exhorts "rest in the Lord; wait for Him" (v. 7, *Amp.*).

This means not only to submit in silence to what He ordains, but also to be ready and expectant for what He is going to do in your life.

Philippians 4:6-9 gives very specific instructions for handling worry. Take a minute to read it. This passage in Philippians can be divided into three basic p's for peace:

- The *premise*: Stop worrying.
- The *practice*: Start praying.
- The *promise*: Peace.

So let's apply these three actions. Take a blank index card and on one side write the word "STOP" in large, bold letters. On the other side write the complete text of Philippians 4:6-9. (Use *The Living Bible* or *The Amplified Bible*.) Keep the card with you at all times. When you begin to worry, find a place to be alone; take the card out; hold the STOP side in front of you, and say, "Stop!" aloud twice with emphasis. Then turn the card over and emphatically read the Scripture passage aloud twice.

Taking the card out interrupts your thought pattern of worry. Saying the word "Stop!" further breaks your automatic habit pattern of worry. Then reading the word of God aloud becomes the positive substitute for worry. (If you are in a group of people and begin to worry, follow the same procedure, only do it silently!)

Freedom from worry *is* possible! It requires that you practice the diligent application of God's Word in your life. This means repetitive behavior. If you fail, don't give up. You may have practiced worrying for many years, and you need to consistently practice the application of Scripture throughout a longer period of time to completely establish a new, worry-free pattern.

QUESTIONS FOR REFLECTION

Do you really want to conquer worry? Will you take responsibility for guarding your own heart? If so, why not take the time now to create your own STOP sign?

18

Speaking the Truth in Love

But speaking the truth in love, we are to grow up in all aspects into Him, who is the head, even Christ.

—EPHESIANS 4:15

Parents have a tough job. They look forward to having a loving beautiful child, but what do they get? A wrinkled, crying machine that takes in food every two hours and lets it out just as fast. Amazingly, parents survive. The child grows and the parents teach, direct, nurture, chauffeur, guide, provide, attend endless rehearsals and games, help with homework, screen boyfriends and girlfriends and hope to survive the hormonally imbalanced teenage years.

Your parents helped to shape and mold you. Then they gently booted you out of the nest so you could fly on your own as an eagle does with its offspring. Or at least they were supposed to!

Some parents, however, find it difficult to relinquish control and direction in the lives of their children. It doesn't matter whether the child is 25, 35 or 40 years old, they never stop being a protective (and controlling) parent. Perhaps you have that kind of parents.

They continue to give you verbal advice. They send you newspaper clippings with articles that fill your spare time with things to read as well as a TV guide with certain (uplifting) programs circled to guide you in seeking wholesome entertainment. They keep trying to meet your needs (all in loving ways) because your welfare is foremost in their minds. They make suggestions, give reminders and would love to have your cellular phone number as well as your beeper number.

Does this sound familiar? Well, if so, you have what is called a "perpetual parent" in your life. This kind of parent short-circuits your ability to be an adult. You probably wish they would back off and give you the space you need to function on your own. It's often difficult, though, to express anger when you feel guilty for not appreciating their seemingly helpful and devoted acts of love.

Perhaps it's not a parent you are having this struggle with; maybe it's another significant person who does too much for you. When people—

no matter who they are—act intrusively helpful, it's normal to feel as though they see you as a nongrown-up adult![1]

So what can you do? Scripture has many things to say about family rules and responsibilities. Let's look at one example:

> While He was still speaking to the multitudes, behold, His mother and brothers were standing outside, seeking to speak to Him. And someone said to Him, "Behold, Your mother and Your brothers are standing outside seeking to speak to You." But He answered the one who was telling Him and said, *"Who is My mother and who are My brothers?"* And stretching out His hand toward His disciples, He said, *"Behold, My mother and My brothers! For whoever does the will of My Father who is in heaven, he is My brother and sister and mother"* (Matt. 12:46-50, italics added).

Interesting! Jesus didn't comply with His mother's request. He chose ministry and adult decisions over family rules. He spoke the truth in love.

Think about this for a moment...How do you respond to significant older people in your life? Is someone setting the rules for you and controlling your life? Is there someone you see as a perpetual parent? Are you responding to anyone as a perpetual parent, even if they are not playing that role? How could you function more as a responsible adult right now?

Some singles have said, "When I marry, then they'll treat me different." This is erroneous thinking. Whatever responses we have chosen before marriage are usually the same after we marry. It's just that after marriage our new spouses are forced to enter the struggle with us.

If you are a single who has believed this lie, you must take responsibility for gently, but firmly, asserting adult responses before you get married.

It will take time, just as all new actions do. However, only if you are willing to take responsibility for the way you respond to the "perpetual parents" and other "perpetual people" in your life will there be change. This will require you to set loving limits on them. It will require you to present yourself to them differently. You will have to avoid responding in a predictable, childlike fashion.

You have been called to be mature and to grow up in all areas of your Christian life. And in doing so, you will have to respond like Jesus!

Who are the people you need to set limits with? What are you afraid of losing by setting those limits? Are you willing to trust God to walk you through this difficult experience so you can serve Him more freely? Why not start today?

Note

1. Roger Hillerstrom, *Rewriting the Family Script* (Grand Rapids, Mich.: Fleming H. Revell, 1995), pp. 97-110, adapted.

19

You and Your Family

For my father and my mother have forsaken me,
but the Lord will take me up.

—PSALM 27:10

Why are you who you are and the way you are today? Just an ordinary run-of-the mill question, right?

Many factors have been combined to make you the multifaceted person you are today. You're the product of your family birth order, your neurological structure, your interactions with your mother, father, siblings, etc. The atmosphere of your home, and especially your relationship with your parents, however, probably played the most significant part in shaping your identity and behavior.

If you were raised in a healthy home, you can consider yourself fortunate. These families are called functional families because they function effectively and productively. Functional families have many of the following positive qualities:

- The climate of the home is positive and nonjudgemental.
- Each member of the family is valued and accepted for who he or she is. Individuality is highly regarded.
- Each person is allowed to operate within his or her proper role. A child is allowed to be a child and an adult is an adult.
- Members of the family care for one another through verbal affirmation and healthy physical touch.
- The communication process is healthy, open and direct. There are no double messages.
- Children are released to separate from Mom and Dad in a healthy manner and to make age-appropriate decisions.
- The family enjoys being together. They do not get together out of a sense of obligation.
- Family members can laugh together, and they enjoy life together.
- Family members can share their hopes, dreams, fears and concerns with one another and still be accepted. A healthy level of intimacy exists within the home.

Do these characteristics reflect the home in which you grew up? Why not take the time to evaluate the health of your family by rating each trait on a scale of 1 (never evident) to 10 (always evident). No one scores 10s across the board. But if your score averages 7 or above, you were fortunate to be raised in a functional family.

Unfortunately, many grew up in homes where they lived under the following kinds of conditions:

- Parents have the privilege of dominating and controlling a dependent child.
- Only parents have the right to determine what is right and wrong. They are the ultimate source of knowledge.
- If a mother or father becomes angry with a child, the child is responsible for those feelings.
- A child must always protect and shield his or her parents from others. Sharing what occurs in the home is not permitted.
- A child's feelings have no place in the home.
- It is important to break a child's will as soon as possible.[1]

Let's look at the results of these two kinds of upbringing:

The functional family: Imagine that your life is represented by a cup. When you were born your cup was empty. You had a lot of needs which had to be met, and when you reached adulthood your cup was full or almost full.

The dysfunctional family: Your cup may only be a fourth, a sixth or an eighth full. You entered life with needs that your father and your family should have met, but didn't. The lower the level in your cup, the more you tend to try to fill it from the outside, often with compulsive or addictive behavior. Many adult emotional problems exist simply because people are carrying cups that have never been filled.

All of us have problems at some time in our lives. Some of us handle them in healthy ways, some of us don't. But we must take responsibility for changing the wrong patterns. How much work that will require depends upon the level in our cups.

What's your level? Remember, there *is* a person who can help you fill your cup to overflowing![2] That person is Jesus.

QUESTIONS FOR REFLECTION

What was the level of function or dysfunction in your home?
Have you asked Jesus to help you fill your cup? What steps are
you willing to take to change some of the wrong behaviors you
learned in your home?

Notes

1. Alice Miller, *For Your Own Good* (New York: Farrar, Straus, and Geroux, Inc., 1993), p. 59, adapted.
2. H. Norman Wright, *Always Daddy's Girl* (Ventura, Calif.: Regal Books, 1989), pp. 142-146, adapted.

20

Our Internal Critic

There is therefore now no condemnation for those who are in Christ Jesus. For the law of the Spirit of life in Christ Jesus has set you free from the law of sin and of death.

—ROMANS 8:1,2

Critics! Who needs them! Yet some people actually make a living by being critics: movie critics, music critics, literary critics, etc. Some people in your life have probably appointed themselves critics of you. They just love following you, watching you and listening to you, waiting for you to make some mistake so they can dump on you. The only critic worse than this person is the critic inside of you!

Self-criticism is often developed through unmet expectations of who or what we think we should be. So it's time for a brief quiz:

1. Do you believe there is something inherently wrong or bad about you?
2. Do you believe your adequacy is defined by the approval or disapproval of others? If so, who are these people? Did your father disapprove of you? If so, how does that make you feel?
3. Do you believe your adequacy is tied to how much money you make? Where did this belief originate?
4. Do you believe you must always be right about everything to be adequate or feel good about yourself? Do you believe you will be disapproved of or rejected if you are wrong?
5. Do you believe you are inadequate because you are overly sensitive?
6. Do you believe you are helpless and powerless?
7. Do you believe you must please everyone to be worthwhile?
8. Do you believe your adequacy is tied to how much education you've acquired?
9. Do you believe your adequacy and worth are tied to how you look? How tall or short you are? How fat or thin you are?[1]

Most of us have a critic residing within who significantly influences what we believe about ourselves and how we respond to others.

Your internal critic is like a condemning conscience. It operates on the basis of standards that were developed in response to the real or perceived judgments and evaluations of your parents and other people you admired. Your internal critic is quick to point out when you don't measure up to their standards. Sometimes your critic is like an internal parent who scolds you in the same words and tone your authority figures used.

In their excellent book *Mistaken Identity*, William and Kristi Gaultiere explain the damage your internal critic can do:

> It's your internal parent who has idealistic self-expectations for you and is quick to criticize and condemn you for not being a "good enough Christian." It's the cruel perpetrator of the crime of murdering your self-esteem. It can also cause spiritual havoc in your life because it is the foundation upon which you build your God image. When you internalize negative and punitive attitudes people have expressed toward you, it's natural to expect that others will treat you in the same way. In this case the sound of God's loving voice can easily be distorted through the loud-speaker of your internal critic.[2]

Spend some time reflecting upon the way God views you. Once you do, it will be more difficult to be so hard on yourself. After all, if God sees so much value in you, shouldn't you believe Him?

QUESTIONS FOR REFLECTION

Whose expectations are you trying to live up to? Are you willing to take responsiblity for changing those expectations? Will you agree with God that it is now time to stop condemning yourself (see Rom. 8:1)? What new statements will you use to replace your internal critical parent?

Notes
1. Jordan and Margaret Paul, *If You Really Loved Me* (Minneapolis: Compare Publishers, 1987), pp. 127-128, adapted.
2. William and Kristi Gaultiere, *Mistaken Identity* (Grand Rapids: Fleming H. Revel, 1988), p. 95.

21

Relational Homelessness

*For God so loved the world, that He gave His only
begotten Son, that whoever believes in Him should not
perish, but have eternal life.*

—JOHN 3:16

We are a nation of homeless people. It's not uncommon to see a man dressed in shabby, dirty clothes standing in front of the post office with a cardboard sign that reads: "WILL WORK FOR FOOD" or a family living on the back of the church parking lot in an old parked car. It's also familiar to hear of couples unable to earn enough money to pay for a roof over their heads who move from home to home housesitting or even skipping town before the rent is due. These people are the obvious homeless. But society is also fraught with people who hide their homelessness; they are the relationally homeless.

Many singles suffer from this malady. Just as the physically homeless tend to drift, so do those who are single and relationally homeless. They don't stay long enough in any relationship to get to know or be known by another person. Their drifting patterns cause them to miss out on receiving and giving love. This inability to settle in relationships has been described as emotional "channel surfing." This term means going from one thing or one person to another without ever making a commitment to stay long enough to connect.

Three possible relationships can be affected by this kind of relational instability: our relationships with ourselves, other people and God. This kind of homelessness is produced from a feeling of not belonging and not being capable of giving or receiving love.

Can you identify with these feelings? Perhaps you are one of the homeless who have not yet looked at your reasons for feeling so alone.

When you don't pay your phone bill, it's soon disconnected by the phone company and you are left "out of touch." Being cut off or estranged from yourself is the same kind of feeling. And when that happens, you feel isolated. Internal isolation comes from self-hatred. It causes you to respond to others with counterfeit feelings because you are afraid to be known and fearful that you cannot meet the needs of those around you.

Thus, it feels safer to keep the communication lines disconnected than it does to risk our fears. We may try to make the connection, but the closeness is too threatening, so we pull away.

An internal push-pull kind of struggle happens because the emotionionally homeless person is overeager for friendship, but too frightened to trust. The fear of being known is so great that long-term commitment is out of the question. If you are one of the singles who suffer with this emotional deprivation, you probably feel all alone—even when you are with other people.

Relational homelessness is a reflection of distancing ourselves from the One who knows us best. Even after we have grasped the enormity and depth of God's love for us, we still live with fear in our lives—fear of ourselves, fear of others and fear of God. But we must remember that God designed us. He created us. He has a definite plan and purpose for us.

The answer to being homeless is simple. Come home. Come home to your heavenly Father and accept His love and appreciation for who He created you to be. Allow Him to cover your past mistakes. Embrace the forgiveness that only He can give. When you do this, you will have a new appreciation for who you are and you can be at home with yourself and others.

The man in front of the post office holding the "WILL WORK FOR FOOD" sign always has to move on within a few hours or a few days. But you don't have to work to get close to God, and life with Him is not for a few hours...or a few days or months or years—it's forever.[1]

QUESTIONS FOR REFLECTION

What's the truth about who you really are? Have you ever shared that part of yourself with anyone else? If not, why not? Have you ever forgiven yourself, others and God for the mistakes of your past? What does God's Word say about your acceptability? What would a healthy commitment look like according to God's Word? What is God's commitment to you?

Note

1. Robbie Castleman, *True Love in a World of False Hope* (Downers Grove, Ill.: InterVarsity, 1996), pp. 148-150, adapted.

22.

Relationships That Last

And beyond all these things put on love,
which is the perfect bond of unity.
—COLOSSIANS 3:14

The recipe for every friendship must include one basic ingredient: *agape* love. The word is often used in the Church to describe God's love, but do you understand what it really means in everyday practical terms? How does it apply to a dating relationship or even marriage?

Agape love manifests itself through several characteristics. First, it is an *unconditional love*. It is not based upon performance; it is given in spite of how the other person behaves. This form of real love is an unconditional commitment to an imperfect person. If you do marry, that's what you will commit yourself to.

Agape love is also a transparent love. It is strong enough to allow another person to know the real you. Transparency involves honesty, truth and sharing positive and negative feelings—you know, the hard stuff.

Third, agape is a healing force. To demonstrate the power of this love, let's apply it to a crucial area of any relationship—irritability. Irritability is a barrier that keeps other people at a distance. It is the launching pad for attack, lashing out, anger, sharp words, and resentment. It is the refusal of love.

If you're in a relationship with someone now, consider these questions: Can you be happy with this person if he or she never changes? Are you loving the person standing before you or an imaginary dream? Can you be happy with this person if he or she changes in ways you never dreamed of? A love with its roots in commitment will last through all the pressures and pain of life's disappointments.

Love means to commit yourself without guarantee, to give yourself completely in the hope that your love will produce love in the other person. Love is an act of faith, and whoever is of little faith is also of little love.

Perfect love would be one that gives all and expects nothing. It would, of course, be willing and delighted to take anything that was offered, asking nothing in return. The person who expects nothing and asks nothing can never be deceived or disappointed. It is only when love demands that it brings on pain.[1]

Agape love is unique in that it causes us to seek to meet the needs of the other rather than demanding that our own be met. Our irritability and frustration diminish when we agape another person because we are seeking to fulfill rather than be fulfilled. This is what agape is all about. So now let's examine two simple questions:

Who has ever loved you with agape, and who have you loved with agape love?[2]

QUESTIONS FOR REFLECTION

Do the relationships in your life right now reflect God's unconditional love? Is there anyone in your life who knows the real you? Where do you need to change in the way you love others? Do you have any irritability barriers you need to tear down today?

Notes
1. David L. Leuche, *Relationship Manual* (Columbia, Md.: The Relationship Institute, 1981), p. 3, adapted.
2. H. Norman Wright, *Finding Your Perfect Mate* (Eugene, Oreg.: Harvest House Publishers, 1995), pp. 163-165, adapted.

23

Recovering from Lost Relationships

*Call to Me, and I will answer you, and I will tell you great
and mighty things, which you do not know.*

—JEREMIAH 33:3

Heartbreak, disappointment, loneliness, numbness—these words describe our feelings when we experience broken friendships or broken dating relationships. Additionally, every survivor of a broken relationship is haunted by a residue of fear about future relationships. They ask themselves, *If it happened once, couldn't it happen again? And if it does, am I the problem?*

Some people face breakups head on, learn from them, override their fears, reestablish trust and love again. But others allow their emotional wounds to remain open and fester. They give in to their fears by withdrawing from intimate relationships. They're overly cautious, guarded and judgmental toward others, thus preventing themselves from getting hurt again.

The trauma of lost love relationships is one of life's most painful hurts; the apprehension about loving again is one of life's greatest fears.

When you have trusted another person with your feelings of love and affection, and that relationship ends, your life can feel as though it has come to a standstill. Usually the first love lost is the most painful.

Many who hurt the most are those who are still deeply attached to former dating partners or fiancés and want the relationship to be restored. They feel desperate, totally out of control and willing to do almost anything to keep their partners. But they have no control over the decisions of their loved ones.

Watching a special person slip away without any recourse leaves you feeling empty and impotent. And if the decision to end the relationship was forced upon you, rejection is a major part of the pain.

You may want to reach out again, but once you've been deeply hurt, it's natural to think: *Forget it, the pain is not worth it.*

So, what can you do to recover? Grieve. When you grieve, you have the opportunity to express your feelings of hurt, fear, anxiety, anger, sadness, depression and even guilt. These emotional responses to major loss come in waves that come crashing upon your heart, subside and come again.

Face them, admit them, accept them and express them. Tears will be a part of this expression and tears are God's gift to those who grieve. Never apologize for them. You never have to apologize for a gift from God. If you can cry outwardly be thankful—some can only cry inwardly!

Grief is the opportunity to express your protest at the loss. It is letting out the part of you that needs to say, "I did not want this to happen and I would change it if I could!" Grief allows you to demonstrate against the way this loss has disrupted your life.

Without grief, it is impossible to look forward again.

When a relational loss occurs, your heart can only ask one question: Why? But as the grieving process unfolds, you will be able to ask: *What can I learn through all of this pain?*

So let's look at the steps to recovery:

1. *Change* your relationship with the person you lost. This means learn to exist and function without that person in your life. Readjust your activities and reconstruct your schedule to fill in the gap the loss has created. Expect to have some memories, but decide to live in the present.
2. *Release* the relationship. Say goodbye to what you lost. This can be done with either a mailed or a non-mailed letter.
3. *Forgive* the other person. This means (eventually) forgiving the person for whatever pain you experienced from him or her. And this will take time. With the passage of time will come new opportunites to replace the emotional investment you once had in the person you are now losing.
4. *Connect* with people. Don't try to do this alone. Let others help you. And above all, share everything with God.

For additional help in this area, you may want to read the following: H. Norman Wright, *Recovering from the Losses of Life* (Revell) and Gerald L. Sittser, *A Grace Disguised* (Zondervan).

QUESTIONS FOR REFLECTION

How have the losses of your past affected your relationship with God? Have you allowed yourself to fully grieve all of the lost relationships in your past? Have you or will you allow others to fill the void? What were some of the lessons you learned from your losses? What steps are you willing to take to trust again?

24

Power Failure

But you shall receive power when the
Holy Spirit has come upon you.

—ACTS 1:8

You're at home. Suddenly the lights begin to flicker and dim...everything darkens. The sounds of household machinery come to a halt. An eerie silence drops like a curtain. Questions race through your mind: *Did someone overload the power source? Could it be a fuse? Is there a problem with the local transformer?*

No matter what the cause, a power outage is no fun. When it lasts for an extended period of time, the food rots in the refrigerator, work cannot be done and tempers tend to keep pace with rising temperatures. Your life is totally thrown off course.

Power outages in our lives can usually be traced to a source as well. Who is your power source? Is it you? Your pastor? Your friends? The Lord? Some of us go through life connected to the real power source; others run their lives on a portable battery pack powered by their own energies. And when they do, the battery pack runs out of juice.[1]

We all need a dependable source for power—especially in our spiritual lives. We need something that will outlast any Delco or Energizer battery. And that something is a person. That's right, a person, not an "it." We need the person of the Holy Spirit. Scripture calls Him "the Spirit of truth," and reminds us that "The world cannot accept him, because it neither sees him nor knows him. But you know him, for he lives with you and will be in you" (John 14:17, *NIV*).[2]

In Acts 2:32,33 we read, "God has raised this Jesus to life, and we are all witnesses of the fact. Exalted to the right hand of God, he has received from the Father the promised Holy Spirit and has poured out what you now see and hear" *(NIV)*.

He gives us the gift of power—the Holy Spirit.[3]

The Holy Spirit has knowledge (see 1 Cor. 2:11); a will (see 1 Cor. 12:11); a mind (see Rom. 8:27); and affections (see Rom. 15:30). You can lie to Him (see Acts 5:3,4); insult Him (see Heb. 10:20); and grieve Him (see Eph. 4:30).

John calls Him the helper. He is God inside of you to help you be a man or woman of integrity. You may think you have to handle that business transaction, that irritating business associate or that alluring temptation by yourself, but you don't. The Holy Spirit is there—all the time. He has a job to do.[4]

Have you plugged in to the power source of this person of the trinity? If not would you like to know how?

You get connected when you pray, listen for His answers and read the Word.

Perhaps that sounds like a lot of work for your busy life. But you can pray lying down, sitting, standing, walking, or driving. You can read at any time—invest a minute to read just one verse. Those who begin their day with Jesus realize they are connected to a power source that can't be overloaded and won't run out of juice. That's a source worth plugging into.[5]

You have a choice—you can either stick with your own battery pack or you can choose the real thing!

QUESTIONS FOR REFLECTION

What is the source for your power? Have you spent time in prayer today? What about His Word? Have you taken the time to listen for His answers?

Notes

1. H. Norman Wright, *Quiet Times for Parents* (Eugene, Oreg.: Harvest House Publishers, 1995), May 24, adapted.
2. H. Norman Wright, *With All My Strength* (Ann Arbor, Mich.: Servant Publications, 1996), February 4, adapted.
3. H. Norman Wright, *Quiet Times for Parents* (Eugene, Oreg.: Harvest House Publishers, 1995), May 24, adapted.
4. H. Norman Wright, *With All My Strength* (Ann Arbor, Mich.: Servant Publications, 1996), February 4, adapted.
5. Lloyd John Ogilvie, *Lord of the Loose Ends* (Dallas, Tex.: Word, Inc., 1991), pp. 43-47, adapted.

25

All Stressed Out with Nowhere to Go

Peace I leave with you; My peace I give to you; not as the world gives, do I give to you. Let not your heart be troubled [or stressed].

—JOHN 14:27

Your muscles begin to twinge. Your fingers start to tap and your eye feels like it's about to twitch. You can feel your heartbeat intensifying and your blood pressure rising as your schedule summons you to action: You pick up the cleaning, grab some fast (junk) food and eat it while you're driving, get the car fixed, return three phone calls, prepare the dinner for your small group meeting and then...then the phone call comes with great news! Guess who's dropping in to stay with you for the next week? Just what you needed.

Now that you feel wound up like a rubber band and your guts have been twisted like a pretzel, what do you have? A classic case of twentieth-century stress.

"Stress" is the common, catch-all word used to describe the tension and pressure you feel in overwhelming situations, but it actually pertains to the irritation accompanied by *any* bothersome life situation. The word for stress in Latin is *strictus*. It means "to be drawn tight." Stress is anything that places conflicting or heavy demands upon you. This could be the pattern of your life. And it is the pattern for many singles.

Stressful demands cause your equilibrium to be upset. Your body contains a highly sophisticated defense system that helps you cope with threatening situations and challenging events. When you feel pressure, your body quickly mobilizes its defenses for fight or flight. In the case of stress, your body is flooded with an abundance of adrenaline, which disrupts normal functioning and creates a heightened sense of arousal.

A stressed person is like a rubber band that is being stretched. When the pressure is released, the rubber band returns to normal. But if stretched too much for too long, the rubber begins to lose its elasticity, becomes brittle, develops some cracks and eventually breaks.

Just as each rubber band can tolerate a different amount of pressure before it snaps, people also have varying tolerance levels. What is stressful to one may not be stressful to another. Some get stressed about future events that cannot be avoided; some get uptight after the fact. Others simply have been stretched for so long and so often that they have become brittle and crumble over even the slightest irritation.

Most stress comes from within—from wrapping feelings, thoughts and attitudes around more than we were built for. That's right, our inner responses are the culprits. What we put into our minds and what we think about affects our bodies. Ask yourself: *What are some of the things that affect my daily thought life?*

What is the first thing you listen to on the radio in the morning? What is the last TV program you watch before attempting to sleep at night? The answer to these questions may expose the reason for some of the stress you feel.

Stressful situations are compounded by the way we talk to ourselves when we approach them. The more negative and angry our thoughts and internal talk—*This is awful. This shouldn't be happening. I can't be late. How will I get all this stuff done?*—the more stressed we become.

So how are you feeling right now? Relaxed? Uptight? As you think about the issues facing you today, what is your stress level? If you're feeling stressed, read Psalm 23. This Psalm serves as the Good Shepherd's eviction notice to every stressful thought that might assault your soul:

> He refreshes and restores my life (my self); He leads me in the paths of righteousness [uprightness and right standing with Him—not for my earning it, but] for His name's sake. Yes, though I walk through the [deep, sunless] valley of the shadow of death, I will fear or dread no evil, for You are with me; Your rod [to protect] and Your staff [to guide], they comfort me (vv. 3,4, *Amp.*)

Read this psalm aloud each day for a month and watch the enemy of stress move out of your life.[1]

Where is the stress coming from in your life? Are you attempting to take on more than God has called you to carry? What can you eliminate from your schedule today? Are you adding to your stress level with negative self-talk? Why not begin to practice Psalm 23 today?

Note
1. H. Norman Wright, *With All My Strength* (Ann Arbor, Mich.: Servant Publications, 1996), July 9 and February 4, adapted.

26

Suffering and Grace

Beloved, do not be surprised at the fiery ordeal among
you, which comes upon you for your testing, as though some
strange thing were happening to you; but to the degree
that you share the sufferings of Christ, keep on rejoicing;
so that also at the revelation of His glory, you may
rejoice with exultation.

—1 PETER 4:12,13

Suffering. It's all around us. Most of us begin and end our days reading about it in our local newspapers and hearing about it on the nightly news. We can't get away from it. So we shouldn't be surprised when it happens—we've been warned. Peter warned us that we would have it.

Look again at the scripture for today and read the verses carefully. Did you catch it? Did you see the warning in each verse? Peter tells us we can expect suffering. But notice also, that suffering is followed by joy.

Perhaps you're familiar with the musical presentation of Victor Hugo's *Les Miserables.* It's a story about undeserved grace. It's also a story about a man named Valjean who receives an unjust sentence for stealing a loaf of bread and escapes after spending 19 years in jail.

Both his sentence and suffering were unjust. But he lived in an unjust world. As a result of what he experienced, he became very bitter. His bitterness was only intensified when he discovered what it was like to be an ex-convict in nineteenth-century France. He suffered a life of ongoing rejection. In time, this would have embittered most people.

One night he desperately looks for a place to stay, and is taken into the home of a Catholic bishop. But Valjean takes advantage of the bishop's kindness. During the night he steals most of the bishop's silver. After he leaves, the police catch him and take him back to the bishop's house. Much to the surprise of the police, the bishop hands two silver candlesticks to Valjean saying, "You forgot these." He implies to the police that the silver was a gift.

When the police leave, the bishop looks at Valjean saying, "I have bought your soul for God." And in his merciful act of claiming Valjean for God, Valjean's bitterness finally leaves him.

The rest of Victor Hugo's novel illustrates what happens when a life is redeemed. If anyone had ever had a reason to hate and lash out, it was Valjean. Instead he followed the bishop's example of mercy. Valjean went on to raise an orphan entrusted to him by the child's mother as she lay dying. He spared the life of the parole officer who had spent years tracking him down. He risked his life to save his future son-in-law from death. The remainder of his life was lived with a sense of joy, returning good for evil.

Here was an embittered, miserable man, struggling with suffering he hadn't deserved. Stories similar to Valjean's have been reflected in the lives of people since the beginning of time. But then Valjean had another experience just as undeserved as was his suffering—the grace and mercy he received at the hand of the bishop.[1]

The author of *A Grace Disguised* summed it up when he wrote:

His suffering was undeserved, but so was his redemption.

Like Valjean, I would prefer to take my chances living in a universe in which I get what I do not deserve, both in pain and redemption. It means that I will suffer loss—I already have; but it also means I will receive mercy. I will have to endure the bad I do not deserve; I will also get the good I do not deserve. I dread experiencing undeserved pain, but I also know I will rejoice over God's undeserved grace.[2]

QUESTIONS FOR REFLECTION

*Are you experiencing undeserved pain today? As a single person,
have you suffered the kind of rejection that makes you feel that life
is just not fair? What unfair things have you put others through that
you did not deserve to be released from? What does grace mean to you?
Who do you need to extend grace to today?*

Notes
1. Gerald L. Sittser, *A Grace Disguised* (Grand Rapids, Mich.: Zondervan, 1996), pp. 113-114, adapted.
2. Ibid., pp. 114-115.

27

Where Are You Going?

What profit is there to the worker from that in which
he toils? I said to myself, "God will judge both the righteous
man and the wicked man, for a time for every matter
and for every deed is there."
—ECCLESIASTES 3:9,17

Let me ask you a few personal questions. How old are you? What have you accumulated? What do you hope to accumulate? What have you accomplished? What do you want to achieve within the next 10 years?

"Stop it!" you might be saying. "Enough is enough!" Perhaps you are thinking, *These are heavy questions and I'm just trying to survive one day after another.*

Many singles are just trying to survive and make ends meet. But don't we all want to *accumulate, accomplish* and *achieve?*

Most of us go about life pursuing these three A's in much the same way. We usually *accumulate, accomplish* and *achieve* through our jobs and by the amount of money we earn. That's why many singles seem to "put in" their 60 to 70 hours per week. Why not? Especially when they receive overtime pay. But living to accumulate, accomplish and achieve can become an unhealthy way of life.

If you are a single who is driven by these three A's, let me ask you a few questions: How long will you be able to continue your current pace? Five, 10 or maybe even 20 years? And what will happen if you marry? Will this pattern fit into a healthy marriage? Will it produce children who feel valued and loved? Will it produce the lifetime of memories you want to fill the scrapbooks of your mind during your retirement years?

Think about it. Now reread the scripture for today.

Talk about extremes! One minute the writer of Ecclesiastes seems to be applauding himself, and the next he's in despair and regretting all that he has done. He is looking back after a life of effort and achievement, expressing his emptiness. "It wasn't worth it," he says. What a feeling of futility! Listen with your heart to the regret in his words:

I hated all the things I had toiled for under the sun, because I must leave them to the one who comes after me. And who knows whether he will be a wise man or a fool? Yet he will have control over all the work into which I have poured my effort and skill under the sun (Eccles. 2:18,19, *NIV*).

Have you ever had similar thoughts? Hopefully not. Lest we too experience such feelings of futility, let's take a moment to look at our priorities and our use of time. It's never too late to correct our ways. Dr. James Dobson said:

I have concluded that the accumulation of wealth, even if I could achieve it, is an insufficient reason for living. When I reach the end of my days, a moment or two from now, I must look backward on something more meaningful than the pursuit of houses and land and machines and stocks and bonds. Nor is fame of any lasting benefit. I will consider my earthly existence to have been wasted unless I can recall a loving family, a consistent investment in the lives of people, and an earnest attempt to serve the God who made me. Nothing else makes much sense.[1]

You can start today to protect yourself down the road a bit—to the end of your life. Evaluate the way you are spending your time. Prepare a plan of action that will reflect the life you want to look back on. What do you want to be able to say about your life? How do you want to feel about your life? You can determine that by what you do now. It's not too late.

QUESTIONS FOR REFLECTION

What changes will you need to make to create a balanced life? What do the investments you have made with your time say about what you value most? What action are you willing to take to create a lifetime that is lived without the regret expressed in today's scripture?

Note
1. James C. Dobson, *Straight Talk to Men and Their Wives* (Waco, Tex.: Word Books, 1980), p. 136.

28

Standing Under Pressure

Who are you to judge someone else's servant?
To his own master he stands or falls. And he will stand,
for the Lord is able to make him stand.
—ROMANS 14:4 *(NIV)*

Who knows about your faith and what you believe? Do you have a reputation for standing for righteousness?

It's difficult to live the Christian life in a non-Christian world. At times it can be lonely and painful. But we can do it. God has promised to give us everything we need to win our spiritual battles. We need only trust Him, persevere and maintain our stand for His kingdom. Chuck Swindoll articulates this in the following story:

You may still be single and interested in discovering God's partner for your life. Have you compromised morally, or have you made it clear where you stand? If you have compromised, that explains why you're struggling with such feelings of discouragement. Perhaps not one person you are dating knows where you stand spiritually. If that is true, no wonder you're having such a battle in your intimate life! You have not declared your allegiance. Until you do, you will not stand strong and stable and secure. Don't be afraid to blow the trumpet of your testimony. It is amazing what occurs when you do.

A student on a college campus or a soldier in the military who declares his faith in Jesus Christ is used of God to be a leader for others to rally around. It has also been my observation that those who fail to take a stand are intimidated until they do. But as soon as a stand is taken, it is just beautiful how it disarms the enemy.

The remarkable story of Jim Vaus is such an account. On one occasion years ago, I heard Jim tell about the time he was secretly entangled with the Mickey Cohen gang. What made that rather interesting is that at the same time Jim was also employed by the Los Angeles Police Department. Fun, huh? During that time the

Lord brought Jim Vaus to Himself. It occurred during the 1949 Billy Graham Crusade in Los Angeles. And the conversion was trumpeted across the pages of the newspaper, since Vaus was a fairly notorious individual.

When Jim's allegiance to Christ was declared, naturally the Mafia heard about it. The new convert was then faced with a decision. I will never forget his words, which went something like this: "I was in my home shortly after I had given my testimony at a Billy Graham Crusade. I'd turned the lights out in one room after another. Suddenly, I stopped and looked out in my driveway as two long, black limousines pulled up—very familiar cars." Knowing full well that the mission of those inside the cars was to kill him, Jim prayed, "Lord, my life is in Your hands. I trust You right now." He opened the front door and walked right out in the driveway—no doubt a surprise to the occupants of the limousines. Immediately the doors on both vehicles swung open and several men in three-piece suits stepped out. They stood in a group around Jim as he told them calmly yet directly, "I have trusted Jesus Christ and Him only as my Lord and my Savior. And I can no longer work with you." God marvelously protected him from harm and preserved his life. Jim stood alone, and he stood firm. He didn't hide his faith or deny his Lord. When he declared his allegiance at that threatening moment, God changed the gang's plan to kill him. As his heart pounded in his throat, Jim watched the men return to the limousines and drive away.

This reminds me of one of the greatest promises in all the Proverbs: "When a man's ways are pleasing to the Lord, He makes even his enemies to be at peace with him" (Prov. 16:7).[1]

QUESTIONS FOR REFLECTION

What are some of the fears you have about taking a stand for your belief in God? What is the worst possible thing that could happen to you if you were to face those fears? Will you trust God to help you stand in the stand you take for Him today?

Note

1. Charles R. Swindoll, *Living Above the Level of Mediocrity* (Waco, Tex.: Word Books), pp. 250-251.

29

Hurry Up! Hurry More!

Be anxious for nothing, but in everything by prayer
and supplication with thanksgiving let your
requests be made known to God.

—PHILIPPIANS 4:6

Hectic, hurried and hassled. Did you ever have one of those days when you just couldn't stop for a minute for fear you would have been run over? When the circumstances of your day—deadlines, dishes, doctors and duties of all kinds—kept shoving you from behind, pushing you with such intensity that it was all you could do to keep from stumbling over your own two feet?

On one of those days it seems that everyone and everything wants a piece of you—especially if you live alone and have to do everything yourself. You feel if you hesitated for just a moment, your circumstances would devour you. You feel frantic, like a chipmunk running around the wheel inside its cage, going faster and faster, but stopping at a place that is no farther along than the place where you started.

At times such as this, it's common to ask, "Will it ever end? Where will I find more time? What else can go wrong? How can I hurry up to hurry more?"

Frantic people are difficult to be around, even if they are Christians. And as Christians we were not called to live like this. Tim Hansel puts it well:

We are called to be faithful, not frantic. If we are to meet the challenges of today, there must be integrity between our words and our lives, and more reliance on the source of our purpose.

"Unless the Lord builds the house, they labor in vain who build it; Unless the Lord guards the city, the watchman stays awake in vain. It is vain for you to rise up early, to sit up late, to eat the bread of sorrows; for so He gives His beloved sleep." (Ps. 127:1,2, *NKJV*).

Almost all Christianity reveals itself in feverish work, excessive hurry and exhaustion. I believe the enemy has done an effective job of convincing us that unless a person is worn to a frazzle, running here and there, he or she cannot possibly be a dedicated, sacrificing, spiritual Christian. Perhaps the Seven Deadly Sins have recruited another member—Overwork.

We need to remember that our strength lies not in hurried efforts and ceaseless long hours, but in our quietness and confidence.

The world today says, "Enough is not enough."

Christ answers softly, "Enough is enough."[1]

Hurrying isn't the answer. It won't help. It won't work. It will only stress you out more and build a sense of panic.

So what can you do? Slow down. This advice may sound paradoxical, but when your day is coming apart and you're running around in circles, stop. Hold everything. Sit down in a comfortable chair, take a deep breath and read the following prayer:

Steady my hurried pace with a vision of the eternal reach of time.

Give me, amid the confusion of the day, the calmness of the everlasting hills.

Break the tensions of my nerves and muscles with the soothing music of the singing streams that live in my memory.

Teach me the art of taking minute vacations—of slowing down to look at a flower, to chat with a friend, to pat a dog, to smile at a child, to read a few lines from a good book.

Slow me down, Lord, and inspire me to send my roots deep into the soil of life's enduring values, that I may grow toward my greater destiny.

Remind me each day that the race is not always to the swift; that there is more to life than increasing its speed.

Let me look upward to the towering oak and know that it grew great and strong because it grew slowly and well.[2]

QUESTIONS FOR REFLECTION

What are some of the pressures facing you today? Have you budgeted your day to allow time to stop, breathe and pray? Why not carry a copy of the prayer you just read to remind yourself that you don't have to hurry up to hurry more?

Notes
1. Tim Hansel, *When I Relax, I Feel Guilty* (Elgin, Ill.: David C. Cook, 1979), p. 55.
2. Charles R. Swindoll, *Strike the Original Match* (Portland, Oreg.: Multnomah Press, 1980), p. 92.

30

Let's Clean House

Yet Thou hast made him a little lower than God,
and dost crown him with glory and majesty!
—PSALM 8:5

Have you ever cleaned house—not the physical structure where you live, but your biological house? You know...your beliefs. They could be out-dated or they could be wrong.

Soiled beliefs are self-punitive. They cause you to be critical about yourself for who you are, what you do, what you don't do, the way you look, where you live, for being single or for not being as responsible as you (or others) think you should be. Soiled beliefs smear your mind with negativity. As one person said:

"I really want to get rid of some of my old beliefs about myself. They do nothing but limit me. I really think it's time to clean house."

Now that's a good beginning, but there's more:

"House cleaning is only half the job—a person also needs to redecorate. Some of the deeply entrenched beliefs may not be easy to dispose of. They will need to be replaced with new, accurate and positive beliefs about self."

It's important that you let go of your past identity which is based on inaccurate messages about you and build a new percep-tion which is based on the unconditional love and acceptance of God. To do so, you need to decide which you value more: your old, false identity or your true, God-given identity. Once you decide which is of greater value, you need to let go of one and grab for the other.

Dr. Paul Tournier compared Christian growth to the experience of swinging from a trapeze. The man on the trapeze clings to the bar because it's his security. When another trapeze bar swings into view, he must release his grip on one bar in order to leap to the other. It's a scary process. Similarly, God is swinging a new trapeze bar into your view. It's a positive, accurate, new identity based on

God's Word. But in order to grasp the new, you must release the old. You may have difficulty relinquishing the familiarity and security of your old identity. But think of what you will gain.[1]

A major element in a positive self-identity is your perception of God. If your view of God is inaccurate, your view of yourself will also be inaccurate. Ideally, your overall response to God, based on a proper perception of Him, will be one of trust. But perhaps that is a struggle for you. Instead, maybe you are angry with God, feeling that He failed to protect you or that He has let you down. Intellectually you may acknowledge that God is the giver of good gifts, but emotionally you perceive Him as the giver of bad gifts.

If this is your situation, you are most likely projecting the unloving characteristics of people who were in authority over you onto God. It's natural to believe that God is going to treat you as they did.

Intensive clinical studies on the development of people's images of God show that our spiritual development of the God image is more of an emotional process than an intellectual one. One psychologist points to the importance of family and other relationships to the development of what she calls our "private God." She maintains, "No child arrives at the 'house of God' without his pet god under his or her arm." And for some of us, the "pet god" we have tied on a leash to our hearts is not very nice, nor is it biblically accurate. This is because our negative images of God are often rooted in our emotional hurts and the destructive patterns of relating to people that we carry with us from our past.[2]

So look inside. What is your real view of God? What are the outdated and soiled beliefs that need to be cleaned up?

QUESTIONS FOR REFLECTION

Do you see God as a loving father who wants to lovingly meet your needs or do you see Him as a tyrant? What are some of the emotions you have had about authority figures from your past that you have transferred onto God? Are you willing to redecorate your internal home with the truth God has provided about Himself in His Word?

Notes
1. Robert S. McGee, *The Search for Significance* (Houston, Tex.: Rapha Publishing, 1987), pp. 84-85, adapted.
2. William and Kristi Gaultiere, *Mistaken Identity* (Grand Rapids: Fleming H. Revell, 1989), p. 56.

31

Seven Mistakes You Can Avoid

Trust in the Lord with all your heart, and do not lean on your own understanding. In all your ways acknowledge Him, and He will make your paths straight.

—PROVERBS 3:5,6

When you drive on any highway, you are bound to see signs of every kind—warning signs. Their purpose is to keep you out of trouble. Unfortunately, not everyone obeys them. There are those who decide to ignore them and do it their own way—not just on highways where we drive our cars, but on the highways of life. When the warning signs are overlooked, accidents occur and often these accidents result in fatalities.

On the highway of life, we commonly pass blissful dating and engaged couples so spellbound with romance that they speed down the road without even glancing at the signs that are posted for their protection. Eventually their marriages result in the pain of unnecessary emotional death and divorce. The sad fact is that most of these tragedies could have been prevented. You might be one of them, or perhaps you are friends with someone who is about to make such a mistake. The following information can be just the roadside service you need.

Neil Clark Warren has identified seven danger signs for faulty mate selection. Carefully study the following warning signs; you will want to obey them:

1. *Slow Down:* The decision to get married can be made too soon. Selecting a life partner is a complex process. It needs to be made with reality and a deep understanding of one another, not with fantasy, idealism and a few good times. Research shows higher levels of satisfaction in marriage when the couple has dated more than two years as compared to those who barely know each other. When you don't know the person long enough, courtship deception can be alive and well.

2. *Wait:* Getting married too young is another factor. But you may be thinking, *Forget it. My concern is that I may be too old if I*

wait! Well, a recent study shows that the most stable marriages have a starting time of 28 years of age. There is hope for those who wait. This does not mean wait until you're so set in your ways that you need a cane to get to the altar. Flexibility and adaptability become a greater struggle with age.

3. *Proceed with Caution:* A problem can occur when one or both are overly eager to get married. Sometimes one is afraid the other will get cold feet, or sometimes both singles are just sick and tired of being alone. Overeagerness often accompanies the grandiose and unrealistic expectations that create a letdown after the wedding.

4. *One-Lane Highway Ahead:* One or both may choose a partner to please someone else. If your pattern in life is to be a pleaser and you try to make everyone else happy, this pattern could carry over into whom you choose for a mate. You don't select a mate to make your friends, siblings or parents happy. No one else has the right or ability to select your life partner. You are the one who must live with that person. Your family and friends have preferences and opinions, but the choice is up to you. Listen to the input of others, but you make your own decision.

5. *Watch Out for Falling Rocks:* If your experience base is limited, watch out. You need to have spent time with this prospective mate in a nondating environment under all kinds of circumstances: working side by side, traveling together on a weeklong mission trip, learning to play together noncompetitively, spending an extensive amount of time with that person's family, seeing him or her function at work and asking and discussing life's hardest questions. Gathering this experience in advance will take away the starry-eyed bliss of infatuation so you don't have to get hit on the head with a rock of truth. Physical attraction alone can only keep your marriage alive for three to five years. Romance can keep it going for five to seven years. But deep friendship and commitment will cause it to last forever.

6. *Dips Ahead:* If you marry with unrealistic expectations, get ready for the big plunge into reality! Evaluate your expectations in advance.

7. *Merge Carefully.* Finally, if either of you have undealt-with personality or behavior problems, you are bringing baggage into the marriage that will interfere with your ability to become one. People who marry to solve their problems and get their

own needs met will eventually find that their selfishness has interfered with their ability to fulfill their mates. Just remember this: "You can't be happily married to another person unless you're happily married to yourself—enough said?"[1]

QUESTIONS FOR REFLECTION

Are you overly eager to find the right mate? If not, do you have a friend who is? Which of these signs are being ignored because you or your friend want to rush to the altar? What changes are you willing to make now so you don't find yourself in an emotional or relational fatality?

Note
1. Neil Clark Warren, *Finding the Love of Your Life* (Colorado Springs: Focus on the Family, 1992), pp. 8-22, adapted.

32

Not Guilty

You know my folly, O God; my guilt is not hidden from you.
—Psalm 69:5 *(NIV)*

There's that twinge again—that little irritating feeling that speaks volumes. You know what it is—guilt.

My guilt has overwhelmed me like a burden too heavy to bear (Ps. 38:4, *NIV*).

Guilt is a feeling of remorse about wrong words or actions. It is a sense of regret because you failed to speak up or do something when you should have or shouldn't have. You'd like to go back and change what you did, but you can't. Neither can you evict that unwelcome tenant, guilt, who moved in when you made the mistake.

Do you remember the first time you felt guilt? It was probably as a child. Then you grew into the adolescent years and even more reasons to feel guilty were added to your life. Some adults carry their childhood and adolescent guilt feelings into their adulthood, and these feelings become quite a burden.

So what about you? What is it that has caused you to feel guilty? And do you really deserve to feel guilty? You see, there is such a thing as false guilt that results from assuming the blame for a wrong done by someone else. Parents sometimes carry this kind of burden for their children. But children can carry it for their parents as well.

God knows about guilt. Often we experience it because we have done something against God. In the Old Testament when a person sinned, he or she bought a lamb as a guilt offering, which meant that the price for the sin was temporarily paid. A priest offered the sacrifice to atone for the person's sin. But Isaiah prophesied that there was coming a Messiah who would become the burnt offering (see Isa. 53:6,10) and that His payment would erase the debt of all who would accept Him.

Your guilt has a positive side. It is a signal to let you know when you've done something wrong. In fact, if you have never felt any guilt, it may mean that you have no conscience. And that's the sign of a psychopathic personality!

Even though most of us do experience guilt, many adults feel like they are on constant trial and that the jury comes back every time with a guilty verdict. Overly sensitive people become their own judges and juries and pronounce undeserved sentences upon themselves. Does that sound like you? If so, Satan is using guilt to lie to you so he can destroy you. But you don't have to listen to his message.

You can counter his attack by following God's plan for guilt:

If we confess our sins, he is faithful and just and will forgive us our sins and purify us from all unrighteousness (1 John 1:9, *NIV*).

Jesus Christ came to take care of the guilt we can't get rid of by ourselves.

Dr. Edwin Cole said:

[E]very person must answer for his or her own actions. And he or she must answer to God alone. That is why Calvary, where Christ died, is so important. It is the only place in the world where sin can be placed and forgiveness from God received. The only place where guilt can be released.[1]

When a person receives a rattlesnake bite or takes poison, the doctor usually gives an antidote to counteract the venom or poison. God has done the same for guilt. That antidote is called grace, which means "unmerited favor." When you accept this wonderful gift, the mantle of guilt that you've been wearing turns to dust.

You can apply this antidote to all of your sins by simply confessing them and receiving His forgiveness today.

QUESTIONS FOR REFLECTION

What are some of the guilt feelings that are seeking to weight you down today? Are you carrying false guilt for something that was done to you? If so, isn't it time to leave that responsibility with the one who needs to assume it? Are you carrying real guilt? If so, what is keeping you from confessing that sin to God and the one you hurt so you can walk in the freedom of forgiveness?

Note
1. Edwin Lewis Cole, *Maximized Manhood* (Springdale, Penn.: Whitaker House, 1981), pp. 118-120.

33

An Exceptional Person

*Do not conform any longer to the pattern of this world,
but be transformed by the renewing of your mind. Then you
will be able to test and approve what God's will is—
his good, pleasing and perfect will.*
—ROMANS 12:2 *(NIV)*

You are an exceptional person. That may be a label you are not familiar with, but it is true.

Christians are people who are called to be "exceptions." We are to be different and stand apart from our society. Most parents want their children to be exceptional. They want their children to do and be the best they can to the fullest of their abilities. Too often, however, they focus only on grades, awards or achievements. Performance is important, but basing our value on what we do rather than who we are is wrong.

Society reinforces this wrong standard by looking to those with top grades and outstanding sports records as exceptional. It places importance on these people regardless of the inward character they do or do not have.

As children of God, we need to be exceptional in character. To do so we must develop character traits that set us apart from the world. Let's look at five of these traits and see how we measure up:

1. Integrity. Our actions need to be consistent with our values. Integrity means we can be depended upon. It means we are trustworthy, and we do what is right in accordance with what we say we believe. Who sees you this way?

2. Credibility. This means we will perform what we said we would do. Credibility means being faithful, and following through. Then others will know they can rely on us. This is critical in our relationship within the Body of Christ as well. Many church single groups have difficulty because some of the people they draw are lacking in integrity as well as credibility. What about you!? Do people know they can trust you to perform what you say you will do?

Recently a story in the sports section of the *Los Angeles Times* told about three exceptional athletes. But one was exceptional in his character.

The article reported that a baseball player who had spit in an umpire's face and received a five-day suspension for his conduct was allowed to play in the play-offs.

It also told of a football player who got away with running a dead ball (one that had already hit the ground) into the goal zone to make a touchdown. The football player reportedly knew the referee had not seen him so he decided to see if he could get away with it. He did.

The last athlete included in this story was a professional golfer who read in the paper that his score the day before was a 73, but he knew that score was wrong—he had signed his score card incorrectly. He called the PGA officials and told them of his mistake knowing this would disqualify him and he would lose about $10,000. This man knew the rules and he abided by them. His act and character were exceptional. What would you have done?

3. Responsibility. We would all benefit from this trait in ourselves as well as others. Responsibility is reflected by commitment and a willingness to do what needs to be done even when it's not our job to do it. Who sees you as responsible?

4. Dependability. People who have this trait follow through and others know it. Dependable people can be taken at their word because what they say they will do, they will get done. They willingly act before being asked. They take initiative. Do others know that you will jump in and get the job done even before you are asked?

5. Tenacity. Tenacious people don't quit; they hang in there. They stay committed. Can you be counted on to keep on going, no matter what the cost?

How have you demonstrated these five character qualities in the day-to-day events of your Christian life? Think about it. Pray about it. The more you develop them, the more exceptional you'll be.[1]

QUESTIONS FOR REFLECTION

Do people know you for your integrity, credibility, responsibility, dependability and tenacity? Which of these traits is most descriptive of you? What actions are you willing to take to become more exceptional?

Note
1. Sheila West, *Beyond Chaos* (Colorado Springs: NavPress, 1991), pp. 137-141, adapted.

34

Accountability to God's People

The good man out of his good treasure brings forth what is good; and the evil man out of his evil treasure brings forth what is evil. And I say to you, that every careless word that men shall speak, they shall render account for it in the day of judgment.

—MATTHEW 12:35,36

There is safety in numbers. That is not only true for our physical protection, but also for our spiritual protection. Spiritually we call this safety in numbers factor "accountability." We don't hear much about this because it's not popular.

Accountability means opening our lives to a few carefully selected trustworthy individuals. Some singles fear doing this because they fear being exploited for their transparency or being gossiped about. Some fear being dominated or controlled by those they've trusted. And these problems can occur if we are not selective in our relationships. But the plus side of taking this relational risk is called Christian growth and support. Chuck Swindoll put it this way:

> The purpose of such a relationship is "to be a helpful sounding board, to guard someone from potential peril, to identify the possibility of a 'blind spot,' to serve in an advisory capacity, bringing perspective and wisdom where such may be lacking."[1]

Accountable relationships require something of us. Let's consider the cost so you can decide whether you are willing to make this kind of a relational investment.

First, you must be willing to be *vulnerable*. This means sharing your wounds, admitting your mistakes and weaknesses when someone calls them to your attention, or better yet, willingly exposing them before they are noticed by others. Proverbs explains:

A man who refuses to admit his mistakes can never be successful.

But if he confesses and forsakes them, he gets another chance (Prov. 28:13, *TLB*).

It is a badge of honor to accept valid criticism (Prov. 25:12, *TLB*).

Another simple quality you will need to muster is *teachability*. This means that you embrace openly rather than defensively the counsel of others, and have a willingness to learn from, hear about and respond to their constructive criticism of you. The book of Proverbs has much to say about teachability:

Teach a wise man, and he will be the wiser; teach a good man, and he will learn more (Prov. 9:9, *TLB*).

Anyone willing to be corrected is on the pathway to life. Anyone refusing has lost his chance (Prov. 10:17, *TLB*).

Hear counsel, receive instruction, and accept correction, that you may be wise in the time to come (Prov. 19:20, *Amp.*).

Women tend to have an easier time with this quality than men do because men often struggle more with overt control issues. Professional fishing guides report that women on their trips usually catch more fish than the men do. Why? It's simple. The women usually listen to the instructions of the guide and follow them. The men don't listen because they want to do it their way!

Another quality required in accountable relationships is *availability*. This means being accessible to others and allowing them to be a part of your life—even if you have to interrupt your routine to make room for them. Being accessible means taking time to listen. Proverbs 17:17 says:

A friend loves at all times.

Finally accountability involves honesty. It requires a commitment to the truth no matter what the personal cost. It practices the words of Ephesians 4:15:

But speaking the truth in love, we are to grow up in all aspects into Him, who is the head, even Christ.

An accountable relationship is one that is without pretense.

If you are willing to pay the price for accountability, you will be one of the select few who knows the true richness of being real in a world that seldom is. We live in an unaccountable society. People have grown accustomed to doing their "own thing." Come to think of it, perhaps that's why we have the problems that are so obvious![2]

QUESTIONS FOR REFLECTION

Do you have friendships that meet the requirement for accountability? Who knows your secret struggles and loves you in spite of them? What steps are you willing to take to be more open with yourself and others?

Notes

1. Charles R. Swindoll, *Living Above the Level of Mediocrity* (Waco, Tex.: Word Books, 1987), p. 127, adapted.
2. Ibid., adapted.

35

Accountability from God's Perspective

So that what was spoken through the prophet might be
fulfilled, saying, "I will open My mouth in parables;
I will utter things hidden since the foundation of the world."
Then He left the multitudes, and went into the house.
And His disciples came to Him, saying, "Explain to
us the parable of the tares of the field."
—MATTHEW 13:35,36

If you are accountable to others, you are in good company. Look at the examples in Scripture: For a time Lot was accountable to his Uncle Abraham, but when he ceased to be accountable, he got in deep trouble! King Saul was accountable to Samuel the prophet. David was accountable to Nathan the prophet. Nehemiah was accountable to the king and Daniel lived in accountability to his peers. Look at the New Testament. Jesus was accountable to God; the disciples were accountable to Jesus. Paul and Barnabus were accountable to the Church at Antioch; Timothy was accountable to Paul. These are just a few of the people Scripture describes who walked in accountability.

As Christians, we don't have a choice as to whether we are to be accountable or not. It's commanded by God:

Be on the alert, stand firm in the faith, act like men, be strong. Let all that you do be done in love. Now I urge you, brethren (you know the household of Stephanas, that they were the first fruits of Achaia, and that they have devoted themselves for ministry to the saints) (1 Cor. 16:13-15).

Now we who are strong ought to bear the weaknesses of those without strength and not just please ourselves. Let each of us please his neighbor for his good, to his edification (Rom. 15:1,2).

Bear one another's burdens, and thus fulfill the law of Christ (Gal. 6:2).

When people in the spotlight or positions of power are unaccountable, problems develop. The healthiest churches and single groups are those where accountability is required.

Is your church or singles group practicing accountability? Who are the people in your life to whom you're accountable—not just with your feelings, but with the real issues of life such as finances, credit, giving to the Church, how you act at work, whether you work too many or too few hours, how you respond to other family members, what you watch on video or internet, magazines you read, etc.

These are private areas but God has given us the gift of accountability to bless our lives. Let's look at three benefits of this gift:

1. When you are regularly accountable, you are less likely to get yourself into deep water.

Through presumption comes nothing but strife, but with those who receive counsel is wisdom. The teaching of the wise is a fountain of life....Poverty and shame will come to him who neglects discipline (Prov. 13:10,14,18).

2. When you are accountable, you are better able to see the whole picture. The counsel of others expands your world.

Iron sharpens iron, so one man sharpens another (Prov. 27:17).

3. Finally, when you are accountable, you are less likely to get away with sinful "poor decisions."

Faithful are the wounds of a friend, but deceitful are the kisses of an enemy (Prov. 27:6).

God gives good gifts to His children. Let's celebrate His wonderful gift of accountability.

QUESTIONS FOR REFLECTION

Have you been erroneously thinking that accountability was an option for the Christian life? What steps are you willing to take to obey God in the area of accountability? If you are serving in the church, who is your ministry accountable to for constructive correction and guidance?

36

Prayer Problems

*And in the same way the Spirit also helps our weakness; for
we do not know how to pray as we should, but the Spirit
Himself intercedes for us with groanings too deep for words.*
—ROMANS 8:26

Prayer can be a struggle. When it is, our responses are often one of the
following:

- The line was busy. Translation: I don't think I got through to God.
- God never answers. Translation: I was too busy talking to hear
  His voice.
- I didn't know what to say. Translation: My mind wandered; I fell
  asleep; I really couldn't articulate my needs.

Consider each one. They represent what AT&T calls the "busy signal."
Busy, busy, busy! When you have spent more time trying to get
through to a person than actually talking to him or her, the experience
can make you feel frustrated.

Many have felt this way about prayer. But God's Word tells us that He
is never too busy to answer our calls. He always hears. He knows what
we are going to say before we even say it. Isaiah said:

Before they call, I will answer; and while they are still speaking, I
will hear (Isa. 65:24).

The busy signal can be frustrating, but there's another problem we
sometimes encounter on the phone that can bring us to the point of
exasperation: receiving a phone call from a person who talks on and on
and on. Picture the following scenario: The person asks a question, then
he or she answers it before you even get your mouth open! You had
something to say, but the person hangs up the phone before you have a
chance to respond. You wonder why they called you in the first place.
You feel violated and discounted by their unwillingness to hear you. Do
you ever wonder if God feels that way when we call Him in prayer?

We cut short some of our conversations with God and often don't bother to wait for His answers after we pray. Consider what Dr. Lloyd John Ogilvie says about that:

> God has more prepared for us than we are prepared to ask. We need to spend as much time seeking what God wants us to ask for as we do asking. Then our asking will be in keeping with His will. The desire to pray is God's gift. Prayer is not to get God's attention, but to focus our attention on Him and what He has to say to us. Don't make prayer a one-way telephone conversation in which you hang up before you listen to what He has to say![1]

Sometimes our struggles with prayer have more to do with our inability to focus than they do with our ability to talk and listen to God. Our minds begin to wander, and even when we are in the place of prayer, we are not really there. This inability to focus can point to a spiritual struggle in our lives. When this happens, we must call upon the Holy Spirit and ask Him to help us to pray.

Review the passage for today and remind yourself of the power available to you when you are weak in prayer. The Holy Spirit is more than able to pick up the slack if you will only ask Him. That is His promise to you today!

QUESTIONS FOR REFLECTION

Do you feel like God's phone lines are always busy when you pray?
Do your prayer times sound more like conversations or monologues?
What are the spiritual struggles you are having with God that keep you from really listening to His voice?

Note

1. Dr. Lloyd John Ogilvie, *God's Best for My Life* (Eugene, Oreg.: Harvest House Publications, 1981), Jan. 8.

37

The Heart God Hears

*Two men went up into the temple to pray, one a Pharisee,
and the other a tax-gatherer. The Pharisee stood and was
praying thus to himself, "God, I thank Thee that I am not like
other people: swindlers, unjust, adulterers, or even like this
tax-gatherer. I fast twice a week; I pay tithes of all that I
get." But the tax-gatherer, standing some distance away, was
even unwilling to lift up his eyes to heaven, but was beating
his breast saying, "God, be merciful to me, the sinner!" I tell
you, this man went down to his house justified rather than
the other; for everyone who exalts himself shall be humbled,
but he who humbles himself shall be exalted.*

—LUKE 18:10-14

We would all like to believe that these two attitudes of the heart relate
more to our friends and family than they do to us. But we all have problems with pride.

Let's expose it by considering the answers to the following questions:

When you pray out loud in a group, whose benefit is the prayer
really for? Who are you most conscious of while you are praying—God or the others around you?

The passage for today is about two men. One was a man who was not
even noted by the crowd. He was praying *to God*. The other was enamored with himself. He put on a show; he was praying *for the benefit of
the crowd*. Who did God hear? The answer is fairly obvious. Dr. Ogilvie,
Chaplain of the United States Senate, had an insightful comment on
these two:

God does not hear a comparative prayer. The Pharisee took the
wrong measurements, comparing himself with the tax collector.
He was looking down on another human being rather than up to
God. He grasped an opportunity to lift himself up by putting
another down. But our status with God is not based on being

better than others. We are to be all that God has gifted us to be. God has given us the only acceptable basis of comparison: Jesus Christ.

God does not hear the prayer that is based merely on externals. The Pharisee's prayer was built on the unstable foundation of *what he had done*, not *what he was*. Both what he did and abstained from doing were on the surface. He had accomplished it all himself. He had no dependence on God for his impeccable life.

Jesus wants us to understand how pride twists and distorts our capacity for self-scrutiny. Our minds were meant to be truth-gathering computers. But prayers such as that of the Pharisee make us ignore reality and forget things that are beneath the surface agenda of our conscious perceptions. Prayers such as this delude us into thinking that we can be right with God because of our own accomplishments and goodness.

The purpose of prayer is to see things as they are: ourselves as we really are, and God as He has revealed Himself to be. God wants us to come to grips with the true person inside us—our hopes and dreams, failures and sins, missed opportunities and potential.[1]

If this Pharisee had prayed a prayer, it would probably have been a "give me" prayer. You know, the kind that focuses on what we want or need or even expect!

In so doing, though, he would have missed another point about prayer. The point is that prayer is communication with the Almighty. And who He is dictates how our prayer needs to begin. The focus isn't on us—it's on Him. Listen to Dr. Ogilvie again:

All great praying begins with adoration. God does not need our praise as much as we need to give it. Praise is like a thermostat that opens the heart to flow in communion with God. Don't hurry through adoration. Everything else depends on it. Tell God what He means to you, pour out your heart in unhurried moments of exultation. Don't forget He is the leader of the conversation. The more we praise the Lord, the more we will be able to think His thoughts after Him throughout our prayer. He loosens the tissues of our brains to become channels of His Spirit.[2]

Why do you pray? Where do you pray? How much time do you spend alone in communication with God? How much of that time do you invest in adoring Him? Which of the two men in today's scriptural reference more accurately describes you?

Notes

1. Dr. Lloyd John Ogilvie, *God's Best for My Life* (Eugene, Oreg.: Harvest House Publications, 1981), May 8, adapted.
2. Dr. Lloyd John Ogilvie, *Praying with Power* (Ventura, Calif.: Regal Books, 1987), pp. 25-26.

38

Prayer and Sex

*Let marriage be held in honor among all, and let
the marriage bed be undefiled.*
—HEBREWS 13:4

The previous readings have focused on the basics of prayer as they apply
to the everyday issues of life. So, here's the big question: How do you
pray about sex? That's right, prayer and sex—they do go together.
Remember, sex was God's idea. His design is for sex to be expressed
within marriage. He created us this way. He understands the struggles
singles have with sex. He also understands the temptations, the pressures
and the lures the world uses to entice us to pervert its use outside of
marriage.

But He has promised:

No temptation has overtaken you but such as is common to man;
and God is faithful, who will not allow you to be tempted beyond
what you are able, but with the temptation will provide the way
of escape also, that you may be able to endure it (1 Cor. 10:13).

Prayer is one of God's provisions for escape. Many singles are so
ashamed of their sexual feelings that they run away from God and fall
into Satan's sexual traps. What about you? Do you see sex as something
you can talk to God about? Read the following powerful words from the
book *Thank God for Sex* and evaluate your attitudes about this wonderful gift.

Lord, some people say sex and religion don't mix;
　　but your Word says sex is good.
Help me to keep it good in my life.
Help me to be open about sex
　　and still protect its mystery.
Help me to see that sex is
　　neither demon nor deity.
Help me not to climb into a fantasy world

of imaginary sexual partners;
Keep me in the real world
    to love the people you have created.
Teach me that my soul does not have to frown
    at sex for me to be a Christian.
It's hard for many people to say,
    "Thank God for sex!"
Because for them sex is more a problem
    than a gift.
They need to know that sex and gospel
    can be linked together again.
They need to hear the good news about sex.
Show me how I can help them.
Thank you, Lord, for making me
    a sexual being.
Thank you for showing me how to treat others
    with trust and love.
Thank you for letting me talk to you about sex.
Thank you that I feel free to say:
    "Thank God for sex!"[1]

QUESTIONS FOR REFLECTION

Are you struggling with sexual temptations today? Do you believe God can be trusted with your feelings about sex? Do you take those feelings to God in prayer? Are you grateful for the way God made you sexually? If not, would you be willing to communicate those feelings to Him right now, so He can show you that He cares?

Note

1. Harry Hollis, Jr., *Thank God for Sex* (Nashville: Broadman, 1975), pp. 12-13.

39

It's What You Do That Counts

But while he was still a long way off, his father saw him, and felt compassion for him, and ran and embraced him, and kissed him.

—LUKE 15:20

Nonverbal expressions don't lie. They are so automatic that few of us ever learn to distort them. They're powerful. Their messages have more impact than spoken words. Even Jesus used them to express Himself. The Bible tells us that He looked upon people with anger. His face reflected compassion. He communicated with a sigh.

What kind of nonverbals are you known for? We all have them—you do too. They are obvious in the way you walk, the way you carry yourself, the way you use your hands and many other expressive gestures you use. Did you know that even your eye movements convey a message? It's true.

If your eyes are looking up to the right when someone is talking to you, it could be that you are formulating a visual image. And if you shift your eyes up to the left, you could be recalling a previous image. But not too many people know about this so don't worry—you're not giving anything away!

We all use nonverbals continuously to express our feelings—everything from delight, to dismay, to satisfaction, to smugness, to consternation and compassion. People believe our nonverbals more than our words. And well they should, because nonverbal communication is the most accurate. Smiles, frowns, shrugged shoulders, raised eyebrows, crossed arms, extended arms, hands on hips—like the old song says, "Every little movement has a meaning all its own!"

What do your nonverbals say? Do they communicate the message, "Come to me, I love you. I want you close to me. I accept you"? Or do they say, "Don't bother me. I don't want you near me. I'm threatened by you. I don't forgive you"?

In the parable of the drifting son (see Luke 15:11-32), this father demonstrated for each of us how to reach out and accept another person. He did it first through his nonverbals. His wayward son was really not deserving of his father's acceptance. But the father looked up one day and saw the young man dragging himself home. Before his son could grovel for forgiveness, his father got up, ran to him and threw his arms around the dirty, smelly, wayward boy. He accepted him, loved him, and said, "I take you the way you are right now. Welcome back!"

Is there someone you need to welcome back into your life right now through your nonverbal expressions and words? What about a former friend? Someone in your singles group who hurt you? A former dating partner who offended you?

Let's take this questioning one step further and consider your family members. Sibling relationships aren't always the easiest. Is there a brother or sister who is difficult for you to love and accept? What about a mother or father? You may struggle with the issue that they don't deserve your love and forgiveness. That may be true. But that's what forgiveness is all about. You may want the other person to take the first step toward you. Why wait?

Who is it you need to welcome back into your life today? Why not take the risk and extend your arms in love toward a person who is far from you? Each of us in our own way has played the part of the prodigal. And when we turned toward home, God smiled on us. Can we do any less toward those who need acceptance, forgiveness and affirmation?

QUESTIONS FOR REFLECTION

What nonverbals have you been using that need to be changed? What are these nonverbals telling those you interact with about your attitudes toward yourself, God and others? Who do you need to welcome back into your life? What part did you play in the relationship? Would you be willing to reach out to a prodigal for Jesus' sake today?

40

Four Levels of Relationship

Let the word of Christ richly dwell within you, with all wisdom teaching and admonishing one another with psalms and hymns and spiritual songs, singing with thankfulness in your hearts to God.

—COLOSSIANS 3:16

We've all had coworkers or even close relatives who were unpleasant to be around or with whom we just did not "click." Some people are easy to be with and cause us to want to know them more fully. Others we would rather avoid like the plague. In fact, most of us have relatives or in-laws that we probably wouldn't spend any time with were it not for that connection.

What about you? Are you satisfied with the intimacy level of your relationships? Before you decide, examine the following four levels of relationship:

Minimal relationships are simple surface-level verbal interactions that are generally pleasant. People in relationships at this level usually do not give or receive help, emotional support or love. They just speak and listen to each other when necessary. The key to getting along in this level of relationship is to predetermine how much you actually need to interact with this person and then try to make it as positive as possible.

Moderate Relationships contain all the characteristics of a minimal relationship but include one more: giving and sometimes receiving emotional support. There is an openness that enables both parties to listen to each other's hurts, concerns, joys and needs. Ideally, this openness is a two-way street. But even when it is not, believers are called to respond with openness. Moderate relationships occur when one person takes the initial steps toward emotional openness and support. The other person may follow suit or be threatened by the openness. These relationships are usually cautious and take time to build.

Strong relationships can be summed up in one word: "help." A strong relationship develops when a person becomes involved with another by reaching out to minister to that one in tangible ways. People in strong relationships help each other in times of need. For some, the "helping" aspect of the relationship is easier than the emotional. But the truth is that strong relationships need emotional support to survive. When emotional support is neglected, the relationship becomes diluted and shallow.

Quality relationships have all the elements of the previous levels but include the added element of loving trust. Quality relationships cause us to feel safe enough to reveal our inner needs, thoughts and feelings with each other. This level of relationship can exist between friends, parents, siblings and even coworkers. They help us to tear down the walls in our lives rather than build them.[1]

After reading these four levels of relationship, let me ask you a question: Are you satisfied with the intimacy level of your relationships?

QUESTIONS FOR REFLECTION

What do the relationships in your life say about you? Who do you have quality relationships with? Do you reach out to others with trust and vulnerability? If not, why not? What steps are you willing to take today to create better relationships?

Note

1. H. Norman Wright, *With All My Strength* (Ann Arbor, Mich.: Servant Publications, 1996), July 10, adapted.

41

Ambivalent? Me?

Simply let your "Yes" be "Yes," and your "No," "No";
anything beyond this comes from the evil one.
—MATTHEW 5:37, (*NIV*)

Ambivalence has been called many things. Some see it as indecisiveness. Others see it as a fear of being wrong. It's been referred to as the "yes, but" syndrome. It often plagues relationships, especially serious dating relationships. And the older some people get, the more ambivalence seems to become a habit pattern.

When a relationship threatens to transition from a short-term to some kind of long-term relationship, ambivalence can emerge from the woodwork like an infestation of termites. For some, commitment of any kind is very risky. But commitment is never without risk. It requires making a life-changing decision without having all the needed or desired information to make it a sure thing.

A number of singles shared their fears of hesitation about the move to a relationship commitment in the following statements. See if you can identify with some of them:

- If I become too committed, I might lose control of some areas in my life.
- What if I invest in this relationship and she [he] decides to leave me? Is all the pain worth it?
- If I share my strengths and abilities, my partner may see me as controlling or be threatened by my capabilities.
- I might become dissatisfied and unhappy because I may lose some of my freedom and privacy. There are certain parts of my single lifestyle I don't want to give up.
- I may have to give up some of my single friends or activities that I don't share with this person. And some activities this person is involved in are not important to me.
- I like the relationship as it is now. Why rock the boat?
- What happens if I get tied down and someone else comes along? I'll miss out on finding the right one.
- My parents had a lousy marriage. I don't want a repeat of that!

Sometimes ambivalence is called the Approach-Avoidance conflict—a power struggle between the heart and the head. This struggle continues until a conscious decision is made.

Some singles say they haven't committed to a relationship because they are waiting for the perfect person. Guess what? There is not a *perfect person,* nor is there a perfect relationship. Do you feel like this? Then consider this: Suppose you find the perfect person. What is there about you that would cause that person to fall in love with you? That's something to think about!

Have you ever thought of ambivalence as being a form of perfectionism? It can be. And that means you set yourself up for never making a decision because no *perfect* candidates are available. The obstacle of perfectionism will cripple what could have been a workable relationship.

Some call the search for the perfect person the "Frankenstein" syndrome. Dr. Frankenstein tried to create the perfect person, so he gathered outstanding parts from several people. It was an experiment that backfired to say the least.

Another reason for being ambivalent is called the "I'm not good enough" syndrome, which is evidenced by your feelings of unworthiness for a committed relationship. And it means you're not letting the other person make a decision. You may even discount or explain away his or her perception of you.

So, what can you do if you are ambivalent? There are three steps you can take: First, remember that some amount of ambivalence is normal. Second, identify the fears that hold you back. Go to God's Word to discover how you can live a fear-free life. Focus on verses such as, "For God has not given us a spirit of fear" (2 Tim. 1:7, *NKJV*). Finally, if you're moving ahead in a relationship and ambivalence is also moving in, discuss your feelings openly with the other person. That person may be struggling with fear too; the discussion may remove fear's power. It's worth the risk, isn't it?[1]

QUESTIONS FOR REFLECTION

Are you afraid of commitment? What are some of the fears that keep you from fully giving yourself to the relationship? Do you believe God will receive greater glory with or without this person in your life? What steps are you willing to take today to move from ambivalence to commitment?

Note
1. Michael Broder, *The Art of Staying Together* (New York: Avon Books, 1993), pp. 26-28, adapted.

42

Stormy Weather

Let all bitterness and wrath and anger and clamor and slan-
der be put away from you, along with all malice. And be kind
to one another, tender-hearted, forgiving each other, just as
God in Christ also has forgiven you.
—EPHESIANS 4:31,32

Storms come with varying degrees of intensity. Some sweep in unex-
pectedly. Others can be predicted by the formation of the storm
clouds that accompany them. Some storms are minor and just dampen
the ground, while others create havoc, leaving behind permanent
damage.

Relationships also have their stormy times, and when they do, the
people within the relationships have varying degrees of trouble. Every
relationship has advances and retreats, ups and downs, good times and
bad times (or "growth times" as some call them). Some of these
storms can be predicted through the evidence of common factors that
constitute troubled relationships. At times troubled relationships are
a collaboration; at other times they are the result of a one-sided con-
spiracy.

What causes them? Years ago a war movie was released titled *The
Dirty Dozen*. The following are the dirty dozen reasons for stormy relationships:

1. One or both of you have had a background at home with a
   deficit in good relationship modeling. You may have learned
   that the best way to deal with problems was to ignore them or
   retreat. You may lack the skills at this time to resolve conflict.
   You can learn.
2. One or both of you have unrealistic expectations for each other
   and for the relationship. A possibility exists that the two of you
   have never written down your expectations and evaluated them
   together. This is how they're usually resolved.
3. One or both of you are too dependent, or one or both are too
   controlling. If you become dependent upon the other to make

you feel good, worthwhile, valued or in charge, you are in for a rude awakening! This won't work and because it won't, why keep on pursuing an illusional dream? There's a better and healthier way to live.

4. You each love the other, but you don't respect each other. Something has occurred between the two of you that keeps festering just below the surface. When the relationship isn't going well, you dip into this toxic pool and blame your partner for what's happening. Forgiveness isn't a byword for the two of you; and until it becomes one, renewed respect and trust cannot be built.

5. One or both of you have little or no tolerance for frustration. You overreact and each episode seems to intensify. Anger management skills need to be learned.

6. What you like the least about yourself, you tend to project onto the other person. And this is usually translated into anger.

7. One or both of you feel unlovable. If you feel this way, you might be behaving in ways that are self-sabotaging and become a self-fulfilling prophecy. Thus, the issue is never resolved.

8. Some couples thrive on the aftermath of conflict because it is more caring, loving and sensitive. They unconsciously create fights to develop the closeness they desire. If you are arguing much of the time, this could be your problem.

9. A deeper issue is buried alive under the surface, but the fear of talking about it keeps the relationship in constant turmoil. As a result, you fight about unrelated issues.

10. You don't communicate about intimacy. When intimacy needs differ, one will usually end up as a distancer and the other a pursuer.

11. The presence of chemical dependency. Alcohol or drugs can destroy any relationship. The way you behave or communicate while using either will not build your relationship.

12. And finally, if one or both of you feel trapped, major storms will result. Staying in an unhealthy relationship creates more pain than the healthy step of moving forward.

Do any of the dirty dozen apply to your relationship? If so, you may have some decisions to make. It's better to make them now than years down the road.[1]

Are you in a stormy relationship? Which of the dirty dozen reasons are responsible for the trouble you have experienced? What steps are you willing to take to prepare for storms in the future? Is the relationship you now have healthy, or is it time to move on? If it is unhealthy, what personal issues do you need to explore to bring about greater relational health for the future?

Note

1. Michael Broder, *The Art of Staying Together* (New York: Avon Books, 1994), pp. 91-93, adapted.

43

You Can Be a Charismatic Person

(Part 1)

*And Jesus was going about all the cities and the villages,
teaching in their synagogues, and proclaiming the gospel
of the kingdom, and healing every kind of disease and
every kind of sickness. And seeing the multitudes, He felt
compassion for them, because they were distressed and
downcast like sheep without a shepherd. Then He said to
His disciples, "The harvest is plentiful, but the workers are
few. Therefore beseech the Lord of the harvest to send
out workers into His harvest."*

—MATTHEW 9:35-38

Charismatic people. You probably know some. They stand out. They seem special. They have...charisma—a special quality that causes others to respond to them. People listen to them, follow them and want to be around them. You might be wondering, *What is charisma? How do you acquire it? Can you acquire it? Why should you even want to acquire it?*

Charisma is not a pretense or a mask that you put on. It's not a specific kind of hype that you employ. It's a grouping of qualities that make you into a special and unique person. Perhaps one of the best explanations for it comes from John Maxwell:

Charisma is being more concerned about making others feel good about themselves than you are in making them feel good about you.[1]

This sounds like a model for servanthood...and it is. Dr. Maxwell goes on to define the word by using an acrostic to portray the traits of charisma. Keep in mind that these are not inborn traits. They can be developed especially when we turn our lives over to the Lord and let Him work on us from the inside out.

The acrostic John Maxwell uses is:

C oncern
H elp
A ction
R esults
I nfluence
S ensitivity
M otivation
A ffirmation

Now let's look at two of these qualities: concern and help.

"Concern" is the ability to show that you genuinely care about others. Perhaps in your fellowship group at church you've seen two kinds of people. Some arrive with the attitude of "Here I am"; others respond with "There you are."

Think about who you know with these attitudes. Now reread the passage from Matthew. Let's compare these attitudes to that of Jesus. Jesus *went*, He *saw*, He *felt* and He *cared*. As we can discover from Jesus' example, we must spend time with others to discover their needs so we can then respond to them appropriately.

"Help" is simply the ability to reach out. The phone ad "Reach out and touch someone" is a good way to describe this ability. Charismatic people are helpers. They recognize that God's gifts are given to help others:

And since we have gifts that differ according to the grace given to us, let each exercise them accordingly: if prophecy, according to the proportion of his faith (Rom. 12:6).

And He gave some as apostles, and some as prophets, and some as evangelists, and some as pastors and teachers, for the equipping of the saints for the work of service, to the building up of the body of Christ (Eph. 4:11,12).

God has put people in your life who need you to reach out and touch their lives in some way. They need your help—your tangible assistance. A helper often cannot solve another person's problems, but encourages the other person to believe he or she has the capability and ability to solve his or her own difficulties. God has called you to help others; therefore, you may need to loan someone your faith and hope until that one is able to build up his or her own faith. Your belief in someone else may make all the difference in the world.

Who needs your concern today? And who needs your hope and faith?[2]

Are you known as a charismatic person? Do you genuinely care about others and want to help them? Are you willing to loan your faith and encouragement instead of trying to become that person's god by solving that person's problems for them? Are you following Jesus' example to see, feel and care for others today? What can you do to be more like Jesus in caring for others?

Notes
1. John Maxwell, *The Winning Attitude* (Nashville: Thomas Nelson, 1993), p. 34.
2. Ibid., pp. 26-28, adapted.

44

You Can Be a Charismatic Person

(Part 2)

Do nothing from selfishness or empty conceit, but with humility of mind let each of you regard one another as more important than himself.

—PHILIPPIANS 2:3

Charisma! Let's continue our look at this acrostic from the previous selection. You may want review it before reading on. We have already examined "concern" and "help."

The next word in it is "action"—the ability to make things happen. Charismatic people seem to have an aversion to being stagnant. They're definitely not boring! They may be considered unusual, unpredictable or entertaining, but never boring. Surprisingly, they're not all extroverts either! Charismatics make a point of being unique and original in the way they express themselves. They are remembered by others.

One reason they are remembered is that they seek "results"—the next word in our acrostic. These action-oriented people have a way of making things happen. And much of the change they work to create is others-centered. Charismatics want to see others achieve.

They are people of "influence." Sometimes the influence of charismatic people is very apparent; at other times their influence is not obvious until long after they have left the scene. But one thing is for sure: others want to know what these people think.

And not only do these people think and influence greatly, but they have a "sensitivity" to people and changing situations. They sense and feel with their hearts what is the mood or spirit of a situation. Not only can they read people and circumstances well, but they know how to respond to them.

And in responding, they "motivate" others by giving them hope. Charismatics are future-oriented people who refuse to stay stuck in the past. They can usually see a lot of light at the end of the tunnel. The light they see is the result of optimism or hope. These people ignite hope in others.

And finally, people with charisma demonstrate the gift of "affirmation"—encouraging or building up the hopes and hearts of others. First Thessalonians tells all of us to do this: "And we urge you, brethren, admonish the unruly, encourage the fainthearted, help the weak, be patient with all men" (5:14).

During the 1992 and 1994 Winter Olympics, former Olympic skater Scott Hamilton served as one of the commentators for the ice skating events. At one point, Hamilton shared about his special relationship with his mother who had died prior to his winning an Olympic gold medal:

> The first time I skated in the U.S. Nationals, I fell five times. My mother gave me a big hug and said, "It's only your first national. It's no big deal." My mother always let me be me. Three years later I won my first National. She never said, "You can do better," or "Shape up." She just encouraged me.

So how can you become a charismatic person? Begin by following Jesus' example. He was exalted by being a servant and by being humbled:

> Do nothing from selfishness or empty conceit, but with humility of mind let each of you regard one another as more important than himself; do not merely look out for your own personal interests, but also for the interests of others. Have this attitude in yourselves which was also in Christ Jesus, who, although He existed in the form of God, did not regard equality with God a thing to be grasped, but emptied Himself, taking the form of a bond-servant, and being made in the likeness of men (Phil. 2:3-7).

Remember, charisma is being more concerned about making others feel good about themselves than you are in making them feel good about you![1]

QUESTIONS FOR REFLECTION

Are you a charismatic person? Do you genuinely care enough about others to take action? Are you sensitive to their real needs? Do you motivate others with hope and encouragement? What would it take for you to become a charismatic person? Are you willing to pay that price?

Note
1. John Maxwell, *The Winning Attitude* (Nashville: Thomas Nelson, 1993), pp. 30-33, adapted.

45

What Do I Do with My Failure?

*I do not understand what I do. For what I want to
do I do not do, but what I hate I do.*

—ROMANS 7:15 *(NIV)*

"Failure!" The word we dread. Some of us don't allow it in our vocabularies. Failure is what happens to others, or so we would hope to believe. But the truth is that failure is a part of every human life.

We've all failed—some of us more than others. We can all look back at times we wish we could change. Whether it's an "F" engraved on a report card, the hope of a career that did not materialize or the heart-wrenching pain from years invested in a relationship that unraveled at the seams, it hurts.

The word "failure" means "to deceive or disappoint." The words "fallacy" and "fallible" come from the same source. *Webster's Dictionary* says failure is "the condition or fact of not achieving the desired end."[1] But is failure just the absence of success? Is it simply a matter of bombing out, of not completing what we set out to attain? Perhaps not.

Many people have achieved significant goals, but found no satisfaction in them. This too is a side of failure. It's like climbing a path up a mountain and making it to the top, only to find that you have climbed the wrong mountain!

Have you ever felt that way? Have you ever invested in a relationship or a career or a ministry that left you completely disappointed? If so, then you have probably asked the age-old question, Is this all there is?

The answer is no. Failure is not just the pain of a loss, but the pain of a new beginning as well. Failure has much to do with your perspective about it.

When you experience failure, do you judge *yourself* as having failed or what you *did* as having failed? The difference is crucial. You can let failure devastate and cripple you, or you can look for hope in the Scriptures to see how God used people who failed such as Noah, Abraham, Jacob, Moses and others to accomplish His purposes.

Remember, failure is inevitable. It doesn't matter how old you are, how smart you are, how good-looking you are or how spiritual you are—it will happen. Paul went through it. In Romans 7 he talks about it. Years later he said:

> I don't mean to say I am perfect. I haven't learned all I should even yet, but I keep working toward that day when I will finally be all that Christ saved me for and wants me to be. No, dear brothers, I am still not all I should be but I am bringing all my energies to bear on this one thing: Forgetting the past and looking forward to what lies ahead, I strain to reach the end of the race and receive the prize for which God is calling us up to heaven because of what Christ Jesus did for us (Phil. 3:12-14, *TLB*).

Failure reminds us that we are not God! And sometimes we need this reminder! It's when we feel ordinary that God can use us the most. Failure can be God's tool to get our attention when we're stuck and need to move on. It can be the instrument He uses to pry us out of our comfort zones.

Failure is an ingredient for success. Many successful people have said the key to making good decisions in life came from making bad ones.[2]

So, consider this question: What can you do to reconstruct the way you view failure?[3]

QUESTIONS FOR REFLECTION

What are some of the failures that have changed the course of your life?
How has God used them to make you a better person?
What is your attitude about failure? What should it be?

Notes
1. *Webster's New Riverside University Dictionary, 2nd Edition.*
2. Gary Oliver, *How to Get It Right After You've Gotten It Wrong* (Wheaton, Ill.: Victor, 1995), pp. 20-25, adapted.
3. H. Norman Wright, *With All My Strength* (Ann Arbor, Mich.: Servant Publications, 1996), October, adapted.

46

Gripe, Gripe, Gripe

Don't grumble about each other, brothers.
Are you yourselves above criticism? For see!
The great Judge is coming. He is almost here.
[Let him do whatever criticizing must be done].
—JAMES 5:9 *(TLB)*

Griping and complaining are not just twentieth century problems: "The people were soon complaining about all their misfortunes and the Lord heard them" (Num. 11:1, *TLB*). People have been complaining since the fall of humanity.

They gather in homes, offices and churches to fan the flames of negativism. Some act like grumpy bears just coming out of hibernation—from sunrise to sunset, all they do is growl!

Was the home you came from like that? If so, it's anything but healthy. The atmosphere in this kind of home breeds pessimism, bitterness and gloom.

Every family, office and church usually has at least one complainer. Complainers see the worst, look for the problems and then beat them to death by their incessant complaining. Is there anyone in your life that you prefer to avoid because he or she is so negative? If this person is a family member, you're probably stuck with them. If he or she is your employer, you might consider making a change. Anytime you have to exist in an atmosphere where you've got a chronic complainer, the environment is depressive and that depression can be contagious to those who are subjected to it. That may be strong language, but it's true.

Many years ago a comic strip called "L'il Abner" illustrated a character who was a grouch. He walked around with a dark rain cloud over his head even though everyone else stood in the sunshine. Do you know any L'il Abners? Are you one of them?

Every life will have problems, upsets, disappointments, schedule changes, reversals and illnesses. You can't change what happens, but you can change how you respond to your circumstances.

Complaining and griping reinforces our *own* feelings of discontent and negativism.

So what can you do to reverse its effects? Begin each day by finding three reasons to praise and thank God. Write them down, and read your list several times a day. Make a pact with others that when you first see them, you will be positive and uplifting. By making such a commitment for these times, you set the mood for the day to be an encouragement to others. Your positive attitude will infect those around you and help to create a healthy environment.

Even in healthy environments, however, there will be times when you have legitimate complaints. What do you do when you really have a need to share a gripe or complaint? Go ahead, express it. But do it in a way that indicates you want to see change rather than simply criticizing what you don't like.

By the way, these ideas came from people who found that they worked. Let them also work for you.

QUESTIONS FOR REFLECTION

Who is the complainer in your home, office or family? Could it be you?
What steps are you willing to take to change your environment?
Who do you need to make a pact with to maintain a
positive and uplifting attitude?

47

It's *Not* Impossible!

*Call to me and I will answer you and tell you great and
unsearchable things you do not know.*
—JEREMIAH 33:3 *(NIV)*

"Can't be done. Tried it. Just won't work. Nope, it's impossible."

Words and phrases such as these bring progress to a roaring halt and deaden creativity. Experience and knowledge can sometimes cause us to make statements that stifle the learning experiences of life. Some of us seem to have the gift of throwing in the towel—we feel it's a waste of time to try something new. But what would happen if we eliminated words that breed impossibility from our vocabularies. What if we replaced them with a flexible expression such as, "Let's give it a try"?

A few years ago a book was published with the title *Lord of the Impossible*. Each of us have faced obstacles that we thought were impossible. The question is, Do we believe Jesus is Lord of those circumstances?

A young man recently graduated from high school with a high grade point average and an outstanding cross-country track record. When his diploma was awarded to him, he couldn't accept it with his hands because he had none. He was born without any arms, but by the age of five, he had learned to tie his shoes, cut with a pair of scissors and use a computer. His parents believed he could do it. So did he. The word *impossible* wasn't in their vocabulary.

Earlier in this century someone developed the bright idea of creating a parachute. Wouldn't you have loved to have been there when the inventor tried to explain his idea for the first time? Can you imagine the facial expressions and comments of the people around him! The inventor, fortunately, was deaf to the word *impossible*. He tried and yes there were failures, but he kept at it. He persisted. Today parachutes are used to save lives.

You may have a limited perception of what God can do in your life. It may help you to read the following passage aloud each day for a week:

Truly, truly, I say to you, he who believes in Me, the works that I do shall he do also; and greater works than these shall he do; because I go to the Father. And whatever you ask in My name, that will I do, that the Father may be glorified in the Son. If you ask Me anything in My name, I will do it (John 14:12-14).

Have you ever heard the phrase, "The impossible is the untried"? Much of what we experience today in our homes or on the road wouldn't be there if the inventors had listened to people who said, "Impossible!" This is not a word God ever uses to describe our circumstances, so why should we? Instead, He says the opposite: "Try it. Go for it. Let's do it together."[1]

Perhaps you are held back by family members or people at work or church who keep telling you "It's impossible!" Are they really experts?

QUESTIONS FOR REFLECTION

What are the circumstances in your life that you call "impossible"? What new things would you try if failure were impossible? What did God say in John 14:12-14 that you need to apply to your life today?

Notes
1. Jim Goodwin, "The Impossible Is the Untried" in Mark Templeton's *Discovering the Laws of Life* (New York: Continuum, 1994), pp. 31-32, adapted.

48

Emotions

Thy hands made me and fashioned me.
—PSALM 119:73

Emotions! Who needs them? All of us do. Sometimes we have difficulties with our emotions or wonder what possible good they can provide. It's true that anger can wreck a relationship, but it can also serve as a source of energy to do some good. It's true that depression hurts, but it also serves as a message system signaling that something is wrong and needs attention. It's true that fear keeps us unsettled, but it also serves as a warning system to protect us.

Our emotions influence almost every aspect of our lives. God speaks to us through our emotions. They are like a sixth sense. They help us to monitor our needs, make us aware of good and evil, and provide motivation and energy for growth and change. They give us the vigor, power and impetus we need for living.

Because of sin, we usually respond to our emotions in one of two unhealthy ways. First, we deny or ignore them. This response causes us to believe they are unimportant, therefore we dismiss them completely and rely only on our intellect. Our head knowledge becomes deified and we no longer trust our emotions. Emotions, at best, are viewed as unimportant and, at worst, are considered a mark of immaturity.

Men have more of a tendency to hold this belief than women do. Some women, therefore, feel that men were shortchanged. They think men don't have as many emotions as they do or that they have different ones than women do. This is not true. All men and women have the same emotions.

Women, however, are more commonly encouraged to express their emotions, while many men are raised emotionally handicapped for the lack of a male role model who is comfortable expressing emotions. Men are not taught a feeling vocabulary so they often lack the words to explain them.

Unfortunately, when we ignore or minimize the emotional realities of our lives, we distort and limit our perceptions of life. These distorted perceptions keep us from trusting our experiences. Some men and women have learned to repress one or more emotions. But we can't bury something that is alive and expect it to stay buried. When we try, we often tend to deny or ignore the very things God wants to use to help us grow. We can overcome the unhealthy response of denial by learning to express our emotions in words and actions that are constructive rather than destructive.

The second unhealthy response some people have to emotions is to give in to them fully and be controlled by them. This is equally dangerous. This perspective views the intellect as the culprit and defies the emotions. "If I don't feel it, then I can't trust it," is the message of those who embrace emotions *exclusively*. But consider the consequences in the lives of two biblical characters: When Saul allowed his jealousy about David's popularity and success to be in control, he was not able to learn from his mistakes (see 1 Sam. 18-20). Fear and depression caused Elijah to lose perspective and want to die (see 1 Kings 19:4).

Whether you deny or ignore your emotions (option #1) or you embrace them and ignore your intellect (option #2), your response is not healthy.

By God's grace, there is a third option. The healthy response is to view your emotions from God's perspective and to bring them into harmony with your mind. Maturity involves the whole person. It is impossible to be spiritually mature and emotionally immature. True maturity involves bringing balance to your heart, head and will—to your feelings, thoughts and actions. Each aspect of your life is important. Each was designed by God for your good. Each is a manifestation of the image of God in you.[1]

Do you thank God for your emotions? It may be a good start. After all, they are His creation.

QUESTIONS FOR REFLECTION

What emotions are you trying to deny or ignore?
Why? Have you allowed your emotions to control your life?
What steps are you willing to take to create a healthy emotional balance?
Can you think of anyone who would make a good model for you
emotionally? Why not solicit that person's help?

Note
1. Gary Jackson Oliver and H. Norman Wright, *When Anger Hits Home* (Chicago: Moody Press, 1992), p. 65, adapted.

49

You're Not Perfect and That's All Right

*Just as He chose us in Him before the foundation of the world,
that we should be holy and blameless before Him. In love
He predestined us to adoption as sons through Jesus Christ
to Himself, according to the kind intention of His will,
to the praise of the glory of His grace, which He
freely bestowed on us in the Beloved.*

—EPHE_IANS 1:4-6

Perfectionism is a mental monster. That's right. It rages and steals the joy and satisfaction from life.

Do you know any perfectionists? They strive to do the impossible and expect it from others. The standards they set for themselves and others are...forget it! No one could consistently attain them. You're not one of these people, are you?

Some singles never marry because the ugly lie of perfection has robbed them. They're looking for that perfect specimen—the one that exists only in dreams.

Perfectionists have a pet statement: "It could always be better." Things are never good enough—even when they're outstanding. Perfectionists seem to live with tapes inside their heads that continuously play the same message: "It isn't good enough. You must be perfect. If you do better, you'll get some approval. Try harder, but don't make a mistake." And this message is often conveyed to others around them as well.

Perfectionists live by many unspoken rules that have a powerful influence on their lives. These rules create tremendous stress. Three of the most common are:

- I must never make a mistake.
- I must never fail.
- I must play it safe so I always succeed.

Perfectionists are also procrastinators. They don't want to try unless they know they'll be successful. So the job is put off again and again.

Perfectionism is not attainable, nor is it a spiritual calling. We are who we are because of what God has done for us. Read Ephesians 1:4-6. He calls us to live a life of *excellence.* Listen to Kevin Lehman as he describes the difference between the pursuer of excellence and the perfectionist:

- The perfectionist reaches for impossible goals, whereas the pursuer of excellence enjoys meeting high standards that are within his reach.
- The perfectionist bases his value of himself upon his accomplishments, while the person who pursues excellence values himself simply for who he is.
- The perfectionist tends to remember his past mistakes and dwells on them. He is convinced that everyone else remembers them, too. The pursuer of excellence, on the other hand, will correct his mistakes, learn the lessons they have to offer, and then forget about them.[1]

Let's face it, we'll never be perfect here on earth, and perfectionism is not a spiritual calling or gift either. Perfectionistic people strive to be adequate, but they never reach it!

Adequacy is a free gift to us and always has been. God has declared us to be adequate because of what He has done for us through Jesus Christ. Any shortage in our lives has been paid for by God's free gift. We can begin to express ourselves now out of our sense of adequacy instead of striving to become adequate. We can let loose of the criterion of human performance because God calls us to be faithful. This is His standard—faithfulness!

But the drive to be perfect brings with it a strange companion—a high degree of sensitivity to failure. The pain of failure—of doing less than our absolute best—is much greater for perfectionists because they have unrealistic standards. The greater the distance between performance and standards, the higher the degree of pain. Ouch. You may have seen this in your family or your friends or...!

QUESTIONS FOR REFLECTION

Who are the perfectionists in your life? Are you able to detect any of these traits in yourself? If so, are you willing to begin today to replace the tapes of perfectionism with God's standard of adequacy?

Note
1. Kevin Leman, *Measuring Up* (Grand Rapids: Fleming H. Revell, 1988), pp. 165-166.

50

Peacekeeper, Victim or...

Open rebuke is better than love that is hidden.
—PROVERBS 27:5 (AMP.)

Do you ever feel like other people are making your life miserable? Do you ever feel that your freedom of choice has been ripped away? Do other people make your decisions for you? Do you ever think of others as villains? If so, you could be a "peacekeeper-accommodator." If not, you probably know someone who is, so keep reading.

Some think they've been called to a lifestyle of peacekeeping...to an extreme. Scripture does tell us to live in peace with one another since we've been called to peace (see Col. 3:15). But some have gone overboard and become sacrificial lambs. They've become not just peacekeepers, but accommodators who let others walk all over them.

How do you determine the difference between a person who is living according to this biblical principle and the peacekeeper-accommodator who has carried it to extremes? Well...

If you're a peacekeeper-accommodator, you have little tolerance for other people's anger or dissent. You probably feel uncomfortable with an argument and you are bothered when people disagree with you. If you work especially hard to keep the peace, you don't realize the cost. You're constantly watching your step, anticipating and outguessing other people's responses. You act as a censor on yourself to make sure you don't say or do the wrong thing. You live in fear that others might abandon you if you do something wrong.

It is difficult for peacekeeper-accommodators to relax and be at ease in emotionally turbulent conditions. If others sulk, pout or withdraw in any way, they either try to guess what's wrong or chase after them by pampering, coaxing or trying to draw them out. As you read Bobbie Reed's description of what she calls "people pleasers," see if you can identify these characteristics in yourself, your friends or family members:

- People pleasers are addicted to approval and will do almost anything to gain it. If approval is out of the question, they will settle for acceptance or just attention.
- People pleasers generally have low self-esteem in that they do

not consider themselves worthy of being pleased. Adults who have grown up with a desperate need for approval have usually failed to develop either a healthy sense of who they are or a strong sense of self-worth. They have an idea that they probably deserve respect, but they are unable to stand up, speak out or reach for the love and affection they want.

- People pleasers don't believe they will be accepted by others unless they are actively working at winning approval, so they go to extraordinary lengths to win applause. They dress to please. They act to please. They say what they think others want to hear—or they keep their mouths shut, except to compliment others. They spend their hard-earned money on gifts for others. They give more of their time and energy than they can afford to give. They are great self-sacrificers. They live as performers rather than as themselves.

- People pleasers work twice as hard as other people in their relationships. They are usually prompt (not wanting to keep anyone else waiting), gentle listeners (not venturing to express a conflicting opinion) and eager servants ("Please, let *me* do that!"). People pleasers are not pushy, except when smothering others with gifts, favors and helpfulness.[1]

What a way to live! It's not living when we're constantly on guard, denying who we are and putting on a pretense. God calls us to be honest. We are to be people of integrity and not reinforce the negative behavior of others. Did you ever think that a people pleaser contributes to the selfishness of others by letting them have their own way constantly?! Remember, we've been called to exhort, confront and speak the truth in love! Risky? Yes, but a much better way to live.

QUESTIONS FOR REFLECTION

Have you carried peacekeeping to an extreme—are you a peacekeeper-accommodator—are you a "people pleaser"? If so, what steps are you willing to take to be more honest about who you are? If you do not fit into this category, have you found yourself taking advantage of those who do? What steps are you willing to take to help the "people pleasers" in your life find greater freedom?

Note

1. Bobbie Reed, *When Pleasing You Is Destroying Me* (Dallas: Word Publishers, 1992), pp. 14-15.

51

Is Depression a Sin?

*And taking with Him Peter and the two sons of Zebedee,
He began to show grief and distress of mind and
was deeply depressed.*
—MATTHEW 26:37 (AMP.)

Have you ever been depressed? Go on. You can admit it. It's all right.
Everyone gets depressed. Sometimes singles do because they're not married; sometimes marrieds do because they are no longer single.

Most people have very little understanding about depression and often
confuse it with sadness. But sadness is not depression. Sadness is merely
feeling a bit down for a little while. People who are sad can still function.

Depression is different. It lasts longer and is more intense. Its lingering immobilizing intensity causes you to lose perspective, making you
less able to carry on your life's everyday activities. Depression slams
down the window of hope. And sometimes it even draws down a darkened shade.

The loss of perspective that accompanies depression colors the way
you experience your life, your tasks and your family.

When you're depressed, you experience changes in physical activities—eating, sleeping and sex (for those who are married). Some lose
interest in food, while others attempt to set a world record at gorging
themselves. Some sleep constantly; others cannot sleep at all. Whatever
the particular effects, depression interferes with your ability to function.
And when you can function at only 70 percent of your capacity, what
does that do to you emotionally? It creates more depression.

The inability to perform causes your self-esteem to plummet. You feel
less and less positive about yourself as the spiral continues. You question
your own personal value. Self-confidence is low. You withdraw from
others for fear of being rejected. Unfortunately, when you're depressed,
your behavior does draw some rejection from others. You cancel favorite
activities, fail to return phone calls and seek ways to avoid talking with
or seeing others. Not only do you want to avoid people, but you also
desire to escape from problems, and even from life itself. All of this
makes you feel even more isolated as a single person.

When you are depressed, you're oversensitive to what others say and do. It's easy to negatively misinterpret the actions and comments of others. These mistaken perceptions can make you irritable and cause you to either cry easily or become angry.

You have difficulty handling most of your feelings, especially anger. Often this anger is directed outward, against others. But it can also be misdirected toward yourself. When it is, you feel worthless and don't know how to cope. Have you been there? Are you there now?

If so, you probably don't have anyone to talk to about your depression or don't talk with anyone except yourself, which means you are conversing with a depressed person!

Is it abnormal to be depressed? Is depression a sin? Not at all. Depression has been a part of life since the Fall and it will be part of the human experience until we get to heaven.

If you are depressed, you're not alone in it. In fact, you're in good company. Many of the people God used mightily in the Old Testament were so depressed that they wanted to die: Moses, for example, and Job, Elijah, Jonah and writers of the Psalms (see especially Psalms 42 and 43). Our Lord experienced depression in the Garden as He faced the reality of the cross. Great men and women throughout history have struggled with depression. So don't ever let anyone tell you that it's abnormal to be depressed, that it's a sin to be depressed or that Christians don't experience depression. That is just not true!

Depression is a normal response to a negative experience. It's a symptom that warns us we're getting into deep water. Depression is like pain: While pain is inconvenient, it is a warning system, essential for our survival.

So, when you're depressed, listen to the message it has for you. It's there.

QUESTIONS FOR REFLECTION

Can you identify with the human expressions of depression described in today's devotional? Have you been condemning yourself for your depression? Have you believed the lies that you are abnormal or that you are in sin because of these feelings? Will you start today to recognize that the pain of your depression is merely a call for help from the deep pain within? If you are not depressed, will you allow the words you have just read to create compassion in your heart for someone who is drowning in his or her own sea of sorrow?

52

Why Am I So Depressed?

I have set the Lord always before me. Because he is at my
right hand, I will not be shaken....You, O Lord, keep my lamp
burning; my God turns my darkness into light....God is our
refuge and strength, an ever-present help in trouble.
—PSALMS 16:8; 18:28; 46:1 *(NIV)*

The physical and emotional causes for depression can range from repressed anger to guilt to being exhausted or grieving to chemical imbalances.

If you struggle with depression, there are two things you should do: (1) Consult a medical doctor to identify whether or not the depression has a physical source, and (2) read up on the subject to find helpful ways to cope and deal with it.

But for now, let's consider a major cause of depression that everyone experiences: loss.

Loss is often at the heart of depression. Any loss can trigger a reactive depression. Loss can involve something concrete or tangible such as a person, a job, a home, a car, a valued photograph or a pet. The stronger the attachment, the more intense the feelings of loss. Singles often sink into depression over broken engagements, the end of dating relationships and broken friendships that involve explicit trust.

Have you been there? It can feel like the end of the world, and in a physical sense, something or someone is removed from your world.

But there is another potentially devastating kind of loss. It takes place only in your mind—the loss of love, hope, ambition, self-respect or other intangible elements of life. It could even be a dream that disappears or dies.

The most difficult kind of loss to handle, however, is the threatened loss. This loss has not yet occurred, but there is a real possibility that it will. For example: Waiting for the results of a biopsy or a state bar exam, waiting to hear from the admissions office of a college to which you have applied. These situations and many like these carry the possibility of loss. Depression can arise because we feel powerless to do anything about the situation. It is difficult to accept or deal with a loss that has not yet occurred.

Unrealistic expectations can also make us prone to depression. The higher our ideal is above the real, the greater our letdown will be. Unrealistic expectations can be an issue in beliefs about ourselves, others or even our faith. Often they are a factor in relationships with those we date or hope will fall in love with us. And unmentioned expectations can lead to anger, which, if left undealt with, leads to...depression!

When you are depressed, you tend to do two things: First, you withdraw from the Lord and His Word which can give you comfort and support. Second, you become hard on yourself. You see the worst in yourself and may eventually reject yourself.

Reread the verses for today. Read them again and again. Then consider how you feel about yourself as a person. How do you view yourself? Is it the same as how God sees you? Reading God's Word will reveal the truth about who you are and who God is. This truth is the basis for changing your perception of who you are.

Your understanding of who God is and how He wants to work on your behalf will enrich you. It will cause you to realize that He is committed to performing good in your life—even when you feel depressed. Consider what God's Word says about this:

Surely goodness and love will follow me all the days of my life, and I will dwell in the house of the Lord forever (Ps. 23:6, *NIV*).

I will make an everlasting covenant with them: I will never stop doing good to them...I will rejoice in doing them good and will assuredly plant them in this land with all my heart and soul (Jer. 32:40,41, *NIV*).

Let these words lift you up.[1]

QUESTIONS FOR REFLECTION

What are some of the losses you are coping with today? Are they tangible or intangible? Do you find yourself creating unrealistic expectations? Do you believe that God is working on your behalf? What hope can you draw from the Scriptures in today's devotional?

Note

1. H. Norman Wright and Gary J. Oliver, Ph.D., *Good Women Get Angry* (Ann Arbor, Mich.: Servant Publications, 1995), pp. 160-178, adapted.

53

Money and Me

No one can serve two masters; for either he will hate the one and love the other, or he will hold to one and despise the other. You cannot serve God and mammon.

—MATTHEW 6:24

Yes, we're going to talk about money again. We can't afford not to.

God's Word has much to say about money. In fact, there are only about 500 verses in the Bible about prayer, but more than 2,300 about how to handle money and possessions. Jesus summed up the problem of money in the verse for today.

Money can either be used by you, or it can use you. You work all your life for it, but you can't take it with you.

Our world revolves around who has money and how it is used. Poor people have the illusion that money will make them happy. Rich people soon discover that it can't.

Most of us have never thought about, let alone developed, a "money lifestyle." We all have four choices we can make regarding that lifestyle. Some choices have better consequences than others. Which of the following four choices have you made?

You can live *above your means*—it's easy. Anyone can do it. You look rich to other people. You accumulate as much as you want in goods...and pay more than you should in high interest rates. You indulge your insecurities with material goods. The problem is, it's never enough. It takes more...and more...and more.

If as a single all your money goes for what you want, then when you marry you may have a hard time adjusting—especially when children come along. Thus, you begin to live on credit.

Being in debt to someone is not a comfortable feeling. You feel pressure hanging over your head until you can repay what you owe. It is especially sad that today even many singles have experienced financial bankruptcy. Who do you owe money to? Have you made a list recently?

According to Scripture, we were never called to be people in debt: "Let no debt remain outstanding, except the continuing debt to love one another, for he who loves his fellow-man has fulfilled the law" (Rom.

13:8, *NIV*). Of course, it's difficult to purchase a house or other large items without incurring debt. It helps to distinguish whether we really need something or simply want it. Here's a hard question for you: How does this lifestyle glorify God?

Living at your means is a better choice, but still not a good one. Money comes in one hand, but goes out the other at the same rate. At least there is not much debt in this lifestyle. But there are no savings either. The focus is still on gathering rather than on planning for the future. Where do you want to be in five years? What do you want to have in five years? Too often people look back and say, "Where did it go?" Things occupy our thoughts. How does this lifestyle glorify God?

Living within your means is following the scriptural teaching of being a good steward of what God has entrusted to you. If you want to live within your means, you must think about today as well as the future. But more than that, you must consider how your money can be used for the kingdom of God. Tithing is a part of your financial life, even when you can't afford it.

Living below your means is not a typical choice. It requires unusual self-discipline and a deliberate choice not to move up. The gift of giving rather than acquiring is your joy. Money is used only on what is necessary.

Which of these four lifestyles describes your life?[1]

Keep in mind that money is not bad in itself. We all need it. It's useful. But we also need a financial guide for our lives.

Read one chapter a day for the next month from the book of Proverbs. Write down what it says about money. It could change your financial future.

QUESTIONS FOR REFLECTION

Do you use your money, or does your money use you? Where did you learn the money lifestyle you have chosen? Did it develop as you were growing up or since you've been on your own? What were the messages you heard about money as you were raised? Who do you listen to now for guidance about your money? Is tithing a part of your financial lifestyle, even when you can't afford it? What does the way you handle your money say about the importance of God's kingdom in your life?

Note
1. H. Norman Wright, *With All My Strength* (Ann Arbor, Mich.: Servant Publications, 1996), April 26 and May 27, adapted.

54

Who Is Your God?

I have not hidden Thy righteousness within my heart;
I have spoken of Thy faithfulness and Thy salvation;
I have not concealed Thy lovingkindness and
Thy truth from the great congregation.

—PSALM 40:10

You're at work. You've been there long enough to show others that you're a Christian. One day another employee asks, "Who is your God? What is He really like? I've never been to a church, nor have I ever read the Bible. Would you mind describing Him for me so I can understand who He is?" What would you say?

Before you could reply, you would have to answer some questions of your own: Who is my God? What do I believe about Him? What can I tell others about Him that would make them want to know Him, too?

Consider the following:

You were created. At one time you simply did not exist. You just were not! God always has been. He does not have a beginning. He always was and will be.

You need others. You have needs. God does not have any needs. He is self-sufficient and He is complete. He cannot be promoted any higher than He is and He cannot be demoted.

God does not change for the better or the worse. He is perfectly holy right now. His moral character stays the same. The Psalms tell us that He is always the same (see 102:27). God Himself said, "I am the first, I am also the last" (Isa. 48:12).

His character does not change either. One minute you may be loving and kind and the next no one wants to be around you because you are so upset. God is not like that. He is consistent. James 1 explains God's goodness, holiness and generosity as well as His reaction to sin. James says God is one "with whom there is no variation or shadow due to change" (Jas. 1:17, *RSV*).

You can depend on God to be who He is all the time. In Malachi 3:6 we read, "I the, Lord, do not change."

Were you aware that God cannot learn? It's true. He possesses perfect knowledge. He has never learned: "Who has directed the Spirit of the Lord, or as His counselor has informed Him? With whom did He consult and who gave Him understanding?" (Isa. 40:13,14).

This is hard for us to understand because we are always learning. We can't keep up with all we need to learn! God knows everything instantly, and He knows everything equally well. You discover things; God doesn't. You're surprised by things; God isn't. He's not even taken back by anything you think or do. He knows you thoroughly. There is not one thing hidden from God by you. And in spite of this, He loves you just the same. Isn't that reassuring?

In Matthew 6 Jesus says our Father already knows what you need before you ask Him. And there's nothing you can tell God that will shock Him or change His feelings about you. That's good news, isn't it?

One last thought about God: Have you ever heard someone say at church, "Let's go into God's presence and worship Him"? Probably. But that's not correct. God isn't limited by a building. He is everywhere. The Bible teaches that there's no place in heaven or hell where anyone can hide from Him. He is everywhere in the entire world at one time. "The God who made the world and all things in it, since He is Lord of heaven and earth, does not dwell in temples made with hands" (Acts 17:24).

God is love and He loves you. "For God so loved the world, that He gave His only begotten Son, that whoever believes in Him should not perish, but have eternal life" (John 3:16).[1]

So, back to the scene in the office. If you know God in the fullness I have just described, why not share Him with your friend and coworker. Let Him move in with His changeless love to change the people you work with.

QUESTIONS FOR REFLECTION

How well do you know God? How willing are you to share Him with others? Who will you share Him with today?

Note
1. A. W. Tozer, *The Knowledge of the Holy* (New York: Harper and Row, 1961), selected chapter, adapted.

55

What Race
Are You Running?

Yet those who wait for the Lord will gain new strength; they
will mount up with wings like eagles, they will run and not
get tired, they will walk and not become weary.

—ISAIAH 40:31

Some people run for the sheer enjoyment of running. Some run out of necessity. Running takes strength, coordination, energy, endurance and vitality. It takes a risk—both feet leave the ground for a brief moment during each individual stride. Running causes sweat—a lot of sweat.

If you're a runner, then you know that running affects your total body. Your lungs begin to feel like they're going to explode. Your mouth begins to dry out; your tongue feels like sandpaper; your muscles cry out and cramp up; and your heart feels like a drum with a hammer pounding away on it.

Some people do this mile after mile in marathons...and they call it fun! They get a rush, a "natural high" from the experience. Perhaps you are one of them.

Most people, however, do not willingly put themselves through this kind of physical exertion. But all of us as Christians are runners. We've all been asked to run a race. In Hebrews 12:1 we're told to "run with endurance the race."

So where are you in the race? Some people finish the race. Others don't. Some never even leave the starting line. Others get distracted along the way. Some simply run out of steam.

Running the race can be difficult for many reasons. Maybe you are out of shape. This is more than likely your problem if you don't exercise and eat wholesome food. Junk food is insufficient fuel for the body. Not to meddle, but do you have a regular aerobic exercise program that you attend three to four days a week? If so, great. If not, when will you start? It's a great stress reducer as well as a good tool for weight control.

But being out of shape physically is not as bad as being out of shape spiritually. Unfortunately we don't have yellow flashing warning lights on our foreheads such as those on the dashboards of our cars to warn us before running out of gas. Cars run out of gas when we don't put anything in the tanks. It's the same way with our spiritual lives. If we're no further along now than a year ago in our understanding of doctrine, knowledge of Scripture as well as quality and frequency of prayer, how can we be running the race? Our spiritual tanks may be reading "E."

It's also possible to run a race and find ourselves running in the wrong direction. Elijah (see 1 Kings 19) "ran for his life." The problem was that he ran away from God rather than to Him or with Him. What direction are you going? Some Christians get caught up in running a race all right—the rat race. This is a man-made race that drains our energies, has no defined goals and has no defined finish line. It's based on accumulating things. In a rat race, guess who wins? The rat!

We've been called, not to run a rat race, but the Redeemer's race. And there are rewards for those who run it. We don't compete with others in this race—we are free from this pressure. Our only goal is to finish the race, and that comes with endurance. Read the following words from Hebrews to hear what God says about this race:

> Therefore, since we have so great a cloud of witnesses surrounding us, let us also lay aside every encumbrance, and the sin which so easily entangles us, and let us run with endurance the race that is set before us, fixing our eyes on Jesus, the author and perfecter of faith, who for the joy set before Him endured the cross, despising the shame, and has sat down at the right hand of the throne of God (12:1,2).

You *can* finish this race. Recognize God's power. Ask Him for strength as you run each day. If you stray off the course, go back to Him. He'll show you the way.[1]

QUESTIONS FOR REFLECTION

Have you checked your course lately to make sure you are running in the right direction? Is the right Person at your side? What steps do you need to take to fill your tank? What steps do you need to take to get in better shape for the race?

Note
1. Joe B. Brown, *Battle Fatigue* (Nashville: Broadman & Holman, 1995) pp. 27-44, adapted.

56

Preventing Problem Choices

Trust in the Lord with all your heart, and do not lean on your own understanding. In all your ways acknowledge Him, and He will make your paths straight.

—PROVERBS 3:5,6

Early one morning off the Florida coast, the space shuttle Challenger blasted off the platform and began streaking into the sky. Seventy-three seconds into flight, the shuttle exploded. The blue sky came alive with twisted trails of flame and smoke. Large pieces of the shuttle fell toward the ocean. Seven bodies fell as well.

What a tragedy. And like many other tragedies, it happened because of someone's "choice." Someone chose to make a decision—a bad decision. A problem occurred with the O-rings, the circular rubber seals that were supposed to fit snugly into the joints of the sections of the booster engines. The O-rings were critical because they would have prevented gases from leaking at the joints during the launch phase when the rocket was under the greatest pressure and strain. All previous times they had worked. Today they didn't.

But there had been a warning that the O-rings might not work under conditions such as these. The temperature of the weather had dropped below the freezing mark, causing the O-rings to become brittle and inflexible. There were some who warned of the impending danger. But those in authority didn't listen. They made a choice to fly. The result was that the pressurized fuel did leak past the O-rings and ignited.

Why was the decision made? Perhaps it was pride. Perhaps it was the pressure of wanting to stay on schedule no matter what. But it was a bad choice.

Have you ever made choices that blew up in your face? Have you ever made any that you wish you could reverse? Most of us have at one time or another.

We have all made choices that did not turn out well. Sometimes this happens because the decisions we make are not made at the right time.

For example: Cain made a choice during a time he was very *angry*. He chose to kill his brother. Have you ever made a choice when you were angry? If so, what was the result? Did it turn out the way you wanted? What do you wish you would have done differently?

Abraham made a choice to father a child with his servant Hagar during a time of anxiety about his wife's inability to give birth—her childbearing years appeared to be over. What decisions or choices have you made when you were anxious or worried? Were they good decisions, or do you wish you had waited? What will you do the next time?

Moses experienced righteous indignation one day when he saw the way an Egyptian was mistreating a Hebrew. He chose to kill him. Righteous indignation is all right as long as the feeling is pure and the results are constructive. Do you have this feeling toward any situation or person today? If so, how are you choosing to respond?

Saul disobeyed God one day. Why did he make this choice? Because he was impatient. If you ever want to make a poor choice, do it when you're chomping at the bit. You don't think of the consequences, and in time they bite you back.

So...what should you do when you have choices to make? Wait, talk with others, and most important of all—pray. You could avert an O-ring disaster.[1]

QUESTIONS FOR REFLECTION

What are some of the choices facing you today? Are you tempted to make an impulsive decision? What are some of the lessons you have learned from the flippant choices of your past? Do you believe God should be a part of all your choices? If so, in what ways does your life reflect that answer?

Note
1. Gordan MacDonald, *Rebuilding Your Broken World* (Nashville: Thomas Nelson, 1988) pp. 105-107, adapted.

57

The High Call
of Failure

*And let us not lose heart in doing good, for in due time we
shall reap if we do not grow weary.*
—GALATIANS 6:9

One of the highest callings in our lives is failure. But not only does fail-
ing not *sound* good, it doesn't *feel* good either. And yet, failure and
progress go hand in hand. In most cases failure came before the great dis-
coveries.

A failure or a mistake carries with it the opportunity to make a course
correction to get us back on the right track. Those who persevere have
learned this lesson well. They have developed an endurance and an attitude that says, "I'll never give up."

Have you ever seen James Earl Jones in *Field of Dreams*? Remember
the voice of Mufasa, the father lion in *The Lion King*, or the voice of
Darth Vader in the *Star Wars* films? The voice behind those characters
was that of James Earl Jones. He's won three Emmy Awards, two Tony's,
a Golden Globe and a Grammy.

But it wasn't always like that for James Earl Jones. At age 14 he stut-
tered so much that he never spoke in class. He was awkward, shy and a
loner. The trauma of a move created such insecurity for him that he
found it difficult to talk without stuttering. He began to communicate
with others through notes.

Then one day his teacher asked him to read a poem out loud in front
of his classmates. This took courage, but when he overcame his fear and
began to read, the words started to flow. He liked reading aloud and
wanted to do more. So he practiced again and again. Through his speaking ability he won competitions and eventually a college scholarship. For
years he worked playing small roles in off-Broadway productions and
supported himself as a janitor. But he never, never gave up. He admits
that what he learned through his early disappointments and failures
played a major role in who he is today.[1]

Failure will be a part of your life at some time. Perhaps in your relationship with a sibling, parent, at work, at church or in a dating rela-

tionship. We can either live behind our failures or beyond them.

Let's look at some heroes who have lived beyond them.

Have you ever fallen flat on your face? Probably. But have you done it on cold, hard ice? Probably not. Dan Jansen fell. He fell not only in the 1988 Olympics, but also in the 1992 Olympics. Then in the 1994 Olympics, he leaned over a bit too far and his hands brushed the ice. That cost him a medal. He had one last event to skate in—the 1000-meter race. It wasn't really his specialty event. He didn't feel good. Seven competitors had recorded better times than he. And this would be his last Olympic race. He won! And he won it in world record time. Dan Jansen wouldn't give up. He didn't allow discouragement to rule him.

Perhaps you feel as though you've really messed up. You've made some major mistakes. Have you considered how God can take this and bring some good out of it? It is possible.

Alexander Fleming was a research physician who appeared to make a mistake one day. He left a window open and some mold blew in that contaminated a bacteria culture in a dish. He could have thrown his hands up in frustration and discarded the contaminated dish. Instead he decided to observe what would happen to the bacteria. Something did! The mold produced a substance that prevented staphylococcus growth. He named the substance penicillin. It has healed millions. A mistake? Yes. A failure? Not in this case.

You will continue to fail as you go through life. Learn from your failures. Don't give up. And keep in mind that there is only One person who has never failed. He can help you with yours. His name is Jesus.[2]

QUESTIONS FOR REFLECTION

What are some of the failures you face today? Are you beating yourself up for a failure that God wants to turn into an opportunity? Would you be willing to give Him a chance?

Notes

1. Wallace Terry, "When His Sound Was Silenced," *Parade Magazine* (December 25, 1994): 12-13, adapted.

2. Gary Oliver, *How to Get It Right After You've Gotten It Wrong* (Wheaton, Ill.: Victor Books, 1995) pp. 166-173, adapted.

58

What Do You Believe About Adversity?

And because of the surpassing greatness of the revelations, for this reason, to keep me from exalting myself, there was given me a thorn in the flesh, a messenger of Satan to buffet me— to keep me from exalting myself!

—2 CORINTHIANS 12:7

Stand up at a church gathering sometime and ask everyone there what they believe about adversity. You'll get your ears filled. Some of it will be accurate. Some won't. What do you believe about this companion of life?

Let's consider some facts about this lifelong traveling companion that counter what most of us have learned to believe.

First, there is a divine purpose behind all adversity. We can see from today's scripture that Paul understood this. But it probably took some time before he was able to both understand and accept it.

Second, God may or may not choose to let you know the purpose for your adversity. In Paul's case He did. It was to keep him from developing a pride problem. God revealed to Moses why he couldn't enter the Promised Land. He told Joshua why he and his family were defeated at Ai.

Third, God doesn't berate us when we ask Him why or when we ask Him to take the problem away. He expects us to cry out to Him. When we ask why, it's usually not a real question we are asking, but more a cry of protest. Job asked the question 16 times. He never received an answer. Sometimes you won't either. When we don't hear an answer, we learn to live a life of faith.

Fourth, this one may be hard for you—it is for many: Adversity may be a gift from God. Look at our verse again. Paul had the faith to believe that what he had been given was a gift. His gift was to protect him from pride and the problems that might result.

Fifth, God will comfort you in your adversity. Paul probably wanted something different in terms of a response from God. He didn't get it. But he did experience God's comfort. Have there been times when you've looked for His comfort but could not find it? The question may

- 134 -

be, Where were you looking for that comfort? His Word has it. Other believers can give it. Prayers can be a source for it.

Sixth, God may not choose to intervene and change anything at this time. Have you ever cried out, "Lord, why don't you do something?!" Many have.

Joni Eareckson Tada did. She is confined to a wheelchair because of her spinal cord injury. Through this event, a ministry to the disabled has been established that is impacting thousands. Without her experience, this ministry would never have been born.

Jesus told His disciples:

These things I have spoken to you, that in Me you may have peace. In the world you have tribulation, but take courage; I have overcome the world (John 16:33).

Finally, being contented and satisfied does not depend upon the nature of our circumstances. We can choose to be satisfied or dissatisfied under the same set of circumstances. Sometimes we can change where we live or where we work, but often we can't. A change of scenery may seem attractive and may be needed, but may not happen.

Paul was a survivor. No, he was more than just a survivor—he was content. Why? Because he lived his life for the purpose and plan of God. That's what it takes.[1]

Not that I speak from want; for I have learned to be content in whatever circumstances I am. I know how to get along with humble means, and I also know how to live in prosperity; in any and every circumstance I have learned the secret of being filled and going hungry, both of having abundance and suffering need (Phil. 4:11,12).

QUESTIONS FOR REFLECTION

So what have you believed about adversity? What are the circumstances that God is using to protect you from pride? Where have you been looking for comfort? Are you just a survivor or are you content?

Note
1. Charles Stanley, *How To Handle Adversity* (Nashville: Thomas Nelson, 1989), pp. 164-173, adapted.

59

Criticism:
Can You Take It?

*He whose ear listens to the life-giving reproof will dwell
among the wise. He who neglects discipline despises himself,
But he who listens to reproof acquires understanding.*

—PROVERBS 15:31,32

Can you take it? Do you enjoy it? Will you benefit from it? Three important questions to ask yourself about criticism. We all receive it, whether we want it or not. We get it from coworkers, roommates, employers, parents, people at church and those we're attracted to for significant relationships.

Do you enjoy it? Probably not. Does it make you feel better? Probably not. Do you usually say, "You're right. Thanks for telling me"? Probably not. But we need all the help we can get, even though most of the time we resist it.

The Bible talks about the word "reproof," which is a Hebrew word that means "to correct or to convince." Sometimes God uses His Word to correct or convince us; other times He uses people.

The point is that we *are* going to be corrected, so what's the best way to handle criticism? First, we need to understand the difference between constructive and destructive criticism. To do this we must ask:

Is the purpose of the statement being made to me positive in intent—does it build me up? Or is it intended to be negative—to tear me down and hurt me? Look beyond the words that you hear and pick up the attitude of what is being said. A vast difference exists between a kind, gentle attitude and one that is judgmental.

When is the correction given? If it's done publicly, the other person does not have your best interest at heart. Is it given for your personal benefit, or does it come from the other person's personal hurt?

Second, look beyond the criticism and consider who said it. That may help you decide whether you should take what was said to heart or ignore it. Do you respect and value the person's insights and opinions? Does this person have a pattern of criticism? If he or she does, remember that this is *not* a spiritual gift!

Third, watch your own attitude toward the critic. Make sure you don't react and retaliate with criticism. When you do, you allow this person to control you and shape you into his or her own image! You eventually become just like the person you don't want to be!

A healthier way to respond can be found in God's Word:

> For you have been called for this purpose, since Christ also suffered for you, leaving you an example for you to follow in His steps, who committed no sin, nor was any deceit found in His mouth; and while being reviled, He did not revile in return; while suffering, He uttered no threats, but kept entrusting Himself to Him who judges righteously (1 Pet. 2:21-23).

Fourth, keep in mind that everyone will be criticized. You may be criticized because you are a Christian. That's good. It affirms the fact that you are living your life contrary to society's standards. You are called to do this. Remember that Jesus was criticized. He was called a glutton (see Matt. 11:19); a winebibber (see Luke 7:34); a Samaritan (see John 8:48); and a friend of sinners (see Matt. 11:19; Mark 2:16).

Fifth, don't make it a crusade to stick around critical people in an attempt to prove them wrong. It could be a futile waste of energy. The world is filled with plenty of positive and encouraging people—spend your time with them. It will help you keep from being critical.

Remember, when a hawk is attacked by crows, the hawk doesn't counterattack. He just soars higher and higher until the crows tire and leave him alone. Don't battle critical people, rise above them.[1]

Finally, consider the following scriptures:

> Poverty and shame will come to him who neglects discipline, But he who regards reproof will be honored (Prov. 13:18).

> Where is the man who fears the Lord? God will teach him how to choose the best (Ps. 25:12, *TLB*).

QUESTIONS FOR REFLECTION

Are you going through a difficult time of correction? What can you learn from this criticism? Have you considered the source? Are you wasting time trying to win the favor of someone who has a critical spirit? If so, could God be telling you to rise above them?

Note

1. John C. Maxwell, *Be a People Person* (Chicago: Victor Books, 1996), pp. 122-124, adapted.

60

Being a Critic
Is Not a
Spiritual Gift

*So don't criticize each other any more. Try instead to live in
such a way that you will never make your brother stumble by
letting him see you doing something he thinks is wrong.*

—ROMANS 14:13 *(TLB)*

Being a critic is one of the easiest jobs in the world for which to quali-
fy. You know what I'm talking about, don't you? It's where you become
an expert on another person's flawed character and set out to remold,
refashion or reshape it. Some do it constantly, but we all do it occasionally. We may not always verbalize it, but we sure think it.

There are times though when constructive, affirming criticism is necessary. It may even prevent someone from entering into a disaster or
falling into a sin. But there are appropriate rules that need to be applied
when we are called to bring a corrective word to someone. Let's examine some of them together:

First, what is your motive? The goal of criticism is to help, not to
humiliate. Will what you say build you up and make you look better or
will it build up and help the other person? Will your criticism be pleasurable to you or painful? If you get pleasure out of it, you probably
shouldn't be saying anything. If it's painful, you may be on target.

Second, is this issue worth it? Is this an issue that is really worth saying anything about?

Third, be sure you are specific and clear in what you say. In fact the
best way to ever share a criticism is to spend your time talking about the
desired behavior rather than focusing on what you don't like. Any criticism offered should have as its outcome the edification of the other person. All criticism should be solution oriented rather than problem centered.

Fourth, watch out for absolute statements that cause you to point your
finger at the other person. "You always..." or "You never..." are relationship killers.

Fifth, be aware that what bothers us about ourselves is what we often project onto others. It may help to look at what's going on in your own life first. Jesus said:

> Do not judge lest you be judged. For in the way you judge, you will be judged; and by your standard of measure, it will be measured to you. And why do you look at the speck that is in your brother's eye, but do not notice the log that is in your own eye? (Matt. 7:1-3).

Sixth, be sure you attack the problem rather than the person. There is an old story about a sheepherder in Wyoming who watched the behavior of wild animals during the winter. Packs of wolves would sweep into the valley and attack the bands of wild horses. The horses would form a circle with their heads at the center of the circle and kick out at the wolves, driving them away. Then the sheepherder saw the wolves attack a band of wild jackasses. The animals also formed a circle, but they formed it with their heads out toward the wolves. When they began to kick, they ended up kicking one another.

People have a choice between being as smart as a wild horse or as stupid as a wild jackass. They can kick the problem or they kick one another. Ask yourself, *Am I kicking the problem or the person?*

Finally, ask yourself this: *Is there really as much of a problem or difference of opinion here as I think? Am I seeking a real solution or just looking for problems?*

Do you tend to see the dark or the bright side of things? Do you spend a lot of time going over and over problems in your mind? Do you literally create problems in your own mind? The answer to these questions may lie in whether you're an optimist or a pessimist.

Remember, your calling is not to be a critic, but an encourager. God's Word says:

> Therefore encourage one another, and build up one another, just as you also are doing (1 Thess. 5:11).

QUESTIONS FOR REFLECTION

Are you facing a relationship problem today? Are you more centered on the person or the problem? Have you talked to this person in love so God can be glorified with the result? Are you sure you are not projecting the things that you dislike about yourself onto this person? If you find that you are, how do you believe you can start kicking the problem rather than the person?

61

The Best
Gift of All

*And be kind to one another, tender-hearted, forgiving each
other, just as God in Christ also has forgiven you.*

—EPHESIANS 4:32

Everyone needs it, but few receive it. It benefits the giver as much as the
receiver. It helps even the most broken relationships. And you can't buy
it—it can only be freely given. You probably know what it is by now—
forgiveness.

Anyone who enjoys fishing knows what it means to forgive—you let
the other person off the hook. When you forgive you relinquish all—not
some—but all rights to compensation for the wrong the other person did
to you. Forgiveness though is not a feeling, it's a decision that comes
from your heart. Is there someone in your life who needs your forgiveness?

The Bible gives at least 75 different word pictures of forgiveness. The
following word pictures are derived from 80 different usages of the
word "forgiveness" in the Bible. They show us that to forgive is to:

- Turn the key, open the cell door and let the prisoner walk free.
- Write in large letters across a debt, "Nothing owed."
- Pound the gavel in a courtroom and declare, "Not guilty!"
- Shoot an arrow so high and so far that it can never be found
  again.
- Bundle up all the garbage and trash and dispose of it, leaving the
  house clean and fresh.
- Loose the moorings of a ship and release it to the open sea.
- Grant a full pardon to a condemned criminal.
- Relax a stranglehold on a wrestling opponent.
- Sandblast a wall of graffiti, leaving it looking like new.
- Smash a clay pot into a thousand pieces so it can never be
  pieced together again.

Is there someone in your life who needs your forgiveness?[1]

Let's dispel some of the myths about forgiveness by discovering what forgiveness is not:

Forgiveness is not forgetting. God constructed you in such a way that your brain is like a giant computer. Whatever has happened to you is stored in your memory. What happened will always be with you. There are, however, two different ways of remembering. One is to recall the offense or hurt in such a way that it continues to affect you and your relationship with another. Another way of remembering simply says, "Yes, that happened. I know it did, but it no longer affects me. It is a fact of history, but it has no emotional significance or effect."

Forgiveness is not pretending. You cannot ignore the fact that an event occurred. Wishing it never happened will not make it go away. What has been done is done. Becoming a martyr and pretending ignorance of the event does not help the relationship. In fact, your lack of confrontation and reconciliation may encourage the other person to continue or repeat the same act or behavior.

Forgiveness is not bringing up the past. It is easy to bring up past offenses and hurts. Bringing up the past is destructive because:

- There is nothing you can do to change it.
- It takes you away from giving your energy to the present and future.
- It makes you responsible at this point for jeopardizing your relationship.
- Even if you were severely offended, by dwelling on the offense, you place a continuing burden on the relationship.
- It denies the other person the opportunity to change for the better. This behavior also denies the presence and power of the person of Jesus Christ in a life!
- It does little to elevate you in the eyes of others!

Forgiveness is not demanding change before you forgive. If you demand a change or proof of it first, you expose your own faithlessness and unwillingness to believe in the other person.

Yes, that's risky, but what other options do you have?

Now that you know not only what forgiveness is but also what it is not, is there anyone in your life who needs your forgiveness? If so, why not give it? After all, you're a forgiven person too.

What are some of the myths you have believed about forgiveness?
Who are some of the people you need to let off of your hooks?
Have you been waiting for someone else to change before you forgive?
What does this say about you?

Note

1. John Niedes and Thomas M. Thompson, *Forgive and Love Again* (Eugene, Oreg.: Harvest House Publishers, 1991), pp. 62-63.

62

How to Live a Pollution-Free Lifestyle

No temptation has overtaken you but such as is common to man; and God is faithful, who will not allow you to be tempted beyond what you are able, but with the temptation will provide the way of escape also, that you may be able to endure it.

—1 CORINTHIANS 10:13

Life is full of temptation. It's all around us. We're tempted to lie, falsify our income tax returns, gossip and violate our sexual values. But why shouldn't we? That's the way of our world. Everyone seems to do it. Let's face it, we live in a polluted world—morally and ethically.

But God has called Christians to be different. So what can you do to live a pollution-free lifestyle and reflect the person of Jesus Christ within you?

First, make a decision. It may not be easy, but the first step is to *decide* to live a life of purity no matter what the cost. It's an inner decision and commitment that you *choose* to make.

Second, deal with the temptations in your life by taking the offensive against them. Scripture says, "Flee the evil desires of youth" (2 Tim. 2:22). Running away is one way of dealing with them. But you can't always do that. So when you know you're going to have to confront some present or future temptation, plan now exactly what you will do and say. Rehearse it several times and write out your plan. If you wait until the temptation hits before you develop a plan to conquer it, you'll probably lose.

You know where you're the weakest. Plan ahead. Remember the 60-second rule. What you do during the first 60 seconds of the temptation will determine the outcome. When temptation hits, tell yourself, *I've only got 60 seconds!*

The third step you can take is to determine where the line is that you shouldn't cross. Then stay as far away from the line as is possible. Don't play with it. Set up a "no man's or woman's zone." Set your line 10 yards back and determine not to cross that barrier!

It may help to memorize the following:

> According to my earnest expectation and hope, that I shall not be put to shame in anything, but that with all boldness, Christ shall even now, as always, be exalted in my body, whether by life or by death (Phil. 1:20).

Fourth, apply the words of Proverbs 4:23-27 from *The Living Bible*:

> Above all else, guard your affections. For they influence everything else in your life. Spurn the careless kiss of a prostitute. Stay far from her. Look straight ahead; don't even turn your head to look. Watch your step. Stick to the path and be safe. Don't sidetrack; pull back your foot from danger.

A prostitute can be any person, habit or activity that promises you some short-term pleasure for a price. That puts a new light on it, doesn't it?! If you have some thoughts, habits or activities in your life that you've allowed to take control over you and allowed to become more important to you than God, guarding your heart is an important step.

A fifth step is to guard your mind. Peter told us to do the following:

> Therefore, gird your minds for action, keep sober in spirit, fix your hope completely on the grace to be brought to you at the revelation of Jesus Christ (1 Pet. 1:13).

This means to put out and keep out of your mind anything that is going to be detrimental to the growth of your Christian life. Most problems begin with what goes on in the mind.

Finally, guard your eyes. You know what attracts you and then hooks you. Job knew about this problem and said, "I have made a covenant with my eyes" (Job 31:1). David looked too long and got caught up in a fantasy that led to adultery and murder.

So, what do you look at and what would it be best not to look at? You'll have to decide.

God's Word says temptations can be overcome. That's good news![1]

Have you decided to live a life of purity? What are some of the steps you need to take to guard your heart and mind? Are there some areas in your life where you need to develop an escape plan for temptation? Do you have any "no man's or woman's zones" in your life? Is your lifestyle pollution free?

Note

1. Gary Oliver, *How to Get It Right After You've Gotten It Wrong* (Wheaton, Ill.: Victor Books, 1995), pp. 166-173, adapted.

63

Burnout Can Be Prevented

Come to Me, all who are weary and heavy-laden,
and I will give you rest.
—MATTHEW 11:28

Burnout. Does it really exist? Unfortunately it does, even when you're single. Have you ever experienced it, and do you really know what it is?

Let's begin by defining it. Burnout means "to deplete yourself. To exhaust your physical and mental resources. To wear yourself out by excessively striving to reach some unrealistic expectation imposed on you by yourself or others."

A simple explanation of how people respond in burnout can be determined just by analyzing the word itself. The word "burn" brings about the vision of heat, fire, conflagration or anger. Some people become angry at their jobs, their families, their friends or their employers. That anger seethes beneath the surface, ready to boil up and spill over at the slightest provocation.

The second part of the word is "out," which means there is nothing left. It is as though you've checked out of life itself. You give up, claim that nothing can be done and the entire mess is hopeless. You hurt others by doing nothing. Your energy, integrity, care, love and desire are gone. You are running on empty. There's just nothing more to give!

Burnout is a complex process that involves all five major areas of life: physical, intellectual, emotional, social and spiritual.

The *physical* aspect refers to the amount of energy available to do what you need to do and want to do. Burnout's first symptom is an all-around feeling of fatigue. Physical strength is the first to go. Usually people suffering from burnout are not involved in exercise or in a nutrition or stress-reduction program. What about you? Or is that meddling?

The *intellectual* aspect refers to the sharpness with which you think and solve problems. In burnout this ability diminishes. Creativity diminishes, cynicism concerning new approaches increases, and there's no hobby or means of intellectual relaxation. Your brain feels fried!

The *emotional* aspect refers to whether your emotional life is basically positive or negative. Are you optimistic or pessimistic about what is occurring in your life? Are there emotional outlets available other than work? Are you aware of what is happening to you emotionally? If you become overinvested in work, and your work begins to deteriorate, your whole life can begin to go downhill. Depression can set in from the loss of dreams and expectations that have been tied into your work. A balanced life with outside interests provides a buffer against burnout.

The *social* aspect of burnout refers to feelings of isolation rather than feelings of involvement. What kind of social support system do you have? Do you feel free to share your feelings of frustration, anger, fatigue or disillusionment? Do you have anyone who will listen? Unfortunately, when you experience burnout, you often do not want to burden anyone else with your problems, thus creating further isolation.

The *spiritual* aspect refers to the degree of meaning you see in your life. If your expectations about your work have been crushed, you begin to feel a void in your life. Your dream about life or expectations about what God was supposed to do for you may be a source of disappointment.

Some burnout is simply physical. A person is tired of his or her job—of the hours, or of the ineffectiveness of the system. Perhaps you are dealing with this kind of burnout. If so, you can usually recover after a short vacation or just a day off. This kind of burnout can be dealt with by creating a change that brings about a new interest or even variations in your work routine.

What causes it? It's really simple. When you give and give and give and do and do and do and fail to take in, you're a candidate. Your life is out of balance.

The key word is "balance." You've heard of Death Valley, haven't you? It wasn't always a hot desert. It used to be a lake. One day the inlet dried up but the lake continued to give out. With nothing new coming in, it died.

It could happen to you. It's something to think about as you reflect on your life today.

QUESTIONS FOR REFLECTION

What about you? Are you living a balanced Christian life or are you facing physical, intellectual, emotional, social or spiritual burnout? Where do you need to take in more to prevent your life from becoming a Death Valley?

64

Loneliness

For He Himself has said, "I will never desert you,
nor will I ever forsake you."
—HEBREWS 13:5

In their separation from God, Adam and Eve were the first to experience loneliness:

> Adam and Eve slid into the loneliness of their guilt.
> God withdrew into the loneliness of man's rejection.
> Loneliness is the curse of separation.
> Separation is the result of sin.

Loneliness is a feeling of isolation, of standing apart from others. It's a feeling of emptiness; a feeling of loss. It's a craving for intimacy.

Nearly 50 million Americans have been stricken with what some call a new nationwide epidemic of loneliness.

But loneliness can be cured. The following are some guidelines for combating it:

Reestablish fellowship with God.
Jesus Christ has bridged the chasm of separation to bring God and man together again. He is called the Reconciler.

The wedge of distance can only be removed when we acknowledge that sin is the culprit and that Jesus is the remedy.

The only way to get back into the "family" and to enjoy undisturbed oneness is by receiving Jesus, God's Son:

> But as many as received Him, to them He gave the right to become children of God, even to those who believe in His name (John 1:12).

Reexamine relationships with people.
A poor self-image, anger, hostility, selfishness, even body odor or bad breath can injure relationships.

Friendships are damaged when we enter them with a goal to get rather than to give.

Loneliness is often the result of personality quirks that repel people just as flea powder repels fleas. One of the biggest steps a lonely person can take is to ask a trusted friend or counselor the question, Why don't people want to be around me?

Our friends usually know, and if they are truly our friends they will tell us.

Is there more to loneliness than just being alone?

It appears that being alone is seldom the problem.

We all need solitude occasionally.

Solitude and loneliness are not the same.

Loneliness is more a problem of insulation than isolation. Lonely people may spend their lives with others. They may be like Albert Einstein, who said, "It is strange to be known so universally and yet be so lonely."

We all crave a meaningful relationship—the kind that is able to discuss something other than...

food
    jobs
        cars
            and money.

We crave relationships that welcome talk about...

feelings
    failures
        and fears.

We crave relationships that are willing to...

bear burdens
    confess faults
        and encourage one another.

We crave relationships that believe there is something very sacred and very powerful about the gathering of two or three people with Jesus present.

We crave relationships that move beyond companionship to compassion.

We crave relationships that are as interested in "being" as in "doing."

What we all want is a relationship that will permit "being" without "pretending."

We want a relationship that will allow us to speak without needing to choose our words.

We want a relationship that will even permit silence without suspicion. That's intimacy.[1]

How can you build intimacy?

Be sure you are in an intimate church—one that is more concerned about building lives than buildings. Listen to others. Be honest. Guard confidence. Be available. Pray for others. It will work!

QUESTIONS FOR REFLECTION

Have you isolated yourself from God and others? If so, what steps are you willing to take to get reconnected to Him and to His people?
Are you willing to let another person know the real you?
Would you be a safe person to have for a friend? Why?

Note

1. Don Baker, *Lord, I've Got a Problem* (Eugene, Oreg.: Harvest House Publishers, 1988), pp. 13, 15-18.

65

A Sacrificial Love

"And you shall love the Lord your God with all your heart, and with all your soul, and with all your mind, and with all your strength." The second is this, "You shall love your neighbor as yourself." There is no other commandment greater than these.

—MARK 12:30,31

We've all been called to be lovers—lovers of people. Jesus talked about our need to love in today's passage from Mark. We've been called to love others unconditionally—that can be difficult. We've been called to love willfully. This means we love because we want to love another that way. This too can be difficult. We've also been called to love others sacrificially—this means ignoring the "what's in it for me" attitude. It's putting others first. This can be more than difficult, especially because we often do not know the outcome of our actions.

Perhaps you remember the incident. It happened very early on a foggy morning September 22, 1993, over the Big Bayou Canal near Mobile, Alabama. A barge had struck and weakened the railroad bridge just hours before. Even though the incident was reported, there was no time to check for any damage.

Just moments after this freak accident, an Amtrak train, the Sunset Limited traveling from Los Angeles, California, approached this bridge. At 70 miles an hour it carried the 210 passengers onto the bridge. But the bridge didn't hold. All of a sudden several of the locomotive units and passenger cars went over the bridge into the murky, alligator-infested waters below. In the midst of darkness and fog, smoke and fire erupted. It took two hours before any assistance arrived. By that time, the fire and water had taken the lives of 47 people.

There were those among the surviving passengers who reflected the sacrificial love Jesus talked about in Mark 12. Michael Dopheide was a man responsible for saving 30 people. When he was jolted awake, he heard the screams and groans of the injured. He went out an emergency exit into the black waters and coaxed people one by one out of the doomed passenger car. These people had to leap 6 feet into the 20-foot-deep swamp. After each one jumped, Michael grabbed their arms when they surfaced. He pulled the nonswimmers to safety.

He helped to save an elderly lady, a 2-year-old child and an 11-year-old girl with cerebral palsy. He stayed there cold, wet and exhausted until everyone had been rescued. He responded to what others needed rather than his own needs at the time. This was sacrificial love.

But there was another demonstration of sacrificial love that morning that went beyond what many would ever be able to do. The Chanceys were returning home to Florida with their daughter who had cerebral palsy. With water filling their car, the Chanceys pushed their daughter through a window so she could be rescued. She was. But the Chanceys never made it. In the confines of that car they died. They gave up their own lives to save their daughter. This is sacrificial love.

Most of us will probably never be in this kind of situation. But we have the opportunity to love others every day—it could be a difficult family member, a pain-in-the-neck boss, an obnoxious coworker, a cantankerous roommate, a spoiled "possible" life partner or a self-appointed critic in the singles group.

How have you loved any of them unconditionally?

How have you loved any of them willfully?

How have you loved any of them sacrificially?

Difficult? Sure. Sometimes you may not even want to think of loving them this way. Understandable! Impossible to love them this way? No, not really. Why? It's simple. We've been loved this way by Jesus. Let Him love them through you. It can really happen. Even today!

QUESTIONS FOR REFLECTION

Who are some of the hard-to-love people in your life? How can you show sacrificial love to them? Would you be willing to give up your own needs to bring Jesus' love to someone who doesn't deserve it today? Who?

66

Positive Relationships Are Positively Possible

*A man of many friends comes to ruin, but there is a friend
who sticks closer than a brother.*
—PROVERBS 18:24

How many friends do you have? Go ahead—count them. You know who they are. Are they really true friends or merely casual acquaintances? There is a difference.

Actually Proverbs says having a multitude of "friends" or being a "friend" to an abundance of people is a problem. Proverbs says it will bring about ruin!

What you want to have in your life and what you want to be is a friend that is loyal, trustworthy, faithful and dependable. This is a special person.

Think about it for a minute. Who are those special friends in your life? You may have one or a few, but you won't have a lot of them. And you can be a good friend to one or a few, but you won't have the time or energy for a multitude of them.

And speaking of energy, that's a way to evaluate your relationships. A relationship is either going to be a depleting or a replenishing one. You know what a depleting relationship is, don't you? It's a relationship with someone that drains you emotionally and spiritually.

Being around such a person is hard work rather than a joy—it leaves you exhausted and drained. At first a good relationship or friendship may seem possible with someone such as this, but soon it turns into an exercise in depletion. Draining relationships can happen with siblings or parents. They can happen with roommates and even promising dates.

People who deplete you contribute to your problems rather than help you resolve them. Think of yourself as a battery. These people can drain you so much it's difficult to have enough juice left to even get started again. And there's never a tow truck around when you need one to get a jump start either!

What you want is a replenishing relationship—you know, the kind where you're energized and vitalized by being with this person. He or she adds to your life in a positive way. You look forward to being with the person rather than having an "oh no" response when he or she arrives upon the scene.

Look for people who have this potential. Cultivate friendships with them. But before doing that ask yourself a couple of troubling questions: *What kind of friend am I to others? Do I drain them or fill them?*

Have you ever asked anyone to critique your ability to provide friendship? Probably not. But why not? We can all stand some course correction.

If you're the kind of person who replenishes, you will probably draw that kind of person into your life as a friend. But even if you are not, you can become that kind of person. To be such a person and to have the friendship you want, you will need to give...

Commitment to the other person that your relationship will be healthy.

Time for cultivating the relationship—more time than you ever thought it would take.

Sacrifice for the other person. You will have to see life through the eyes of your friend.

Sharing yourself without taking the other for granted. Sharing is the mortar that holds the relationship together.

Encouragement to fill your time with joy. Look for ways to express this that connect with the other person.

Trust which will develop as you *commit,* make *time, sacrifice, share* and *encourage.* Trust is earned but you also have to be willing to invest trust in the other person.

So, there you have it! What about your relationships? Do they reflect these qualities? They're worth building. After all, we weren't created to live our lives as isolates. We need one another. Thank God today for the close friend(s) God has brought into your life.[1]

QUESTIONS FOR REFLECTION

Has your life been brought to ruin through too many unhealthy relationships? Are your friendships depleting or replenishing? Are you the kind of friend who brings something to the friendship rather than looking for what you can get from it? Do your friendships include commitment, time, sacrifice, sharing, encouragement and trust? If not, will you make the investment beginning today?

Note

1. Ronnie W. Floyd, *Choices* (Nashville: Broadman & Holmes, 1994), pp. 170-174, adapted.

67

Hang In There

But the fruit of the Spirit is...patience.
—GALATIANS 5:22

You've probably heard the expression "Hang in there!" A man known by the name Henry Dempsey did just that...literally! He was piloting a committed flight between two small towns on the East coast when he heard a strange noise coming from the back of the plane. He relinquished the controls of the plane to his copilot and went to the back to check out the noise. Henry was surprised to find that the rear door had not been secured prior to takeoff. Just as he noticed this, the plane hit some turbulence and slammed Henry against the door. It flew open, sucking Henry out over the cold ocean thousands of feet below.

The copilot noticed two things: the open door warning light and the fact that Henry had disappeared! He realized what must have happened so he radioed for a helicopter search over that section of the ocean.

After the plane landed, Henry was found all right. But not where they thought he would be. As Henry was being sucked out the door, he grabbed the outside ladder and hung on for dear life...his own. He was able to hang on despite the plane's descent of several thousand feet at 200 miles per hour. And during the landing he had a bird's-eye view of the runway because he kept his head raised just 12 inches away from the ground.

One last thing about Henry...they had to pry his fingers away from the ladder. This man really "hung in there"!

Sometimes it's difficult to hang in there—especially when we hit the turbulence in our own lives. We'd rather bail out instead of working it out. We're so selective (some call it picky) when it comes to looking for a life partner that at the first upset we say, "I'm out of here" rather than staying and working it out.

When there's difficulty at work, we head for the want ads. When our roommates don't take care of their responsibilities, we're ready to spring the eviction notices.

Sure, life is unfair. Some people are difficult to get along with. But hanging in there and resolving may be a better solution than bailing out. God's Word talks to us time and time again about patience, endurance and sticking it out! Consider the following scriptures:

He who is slow to anger has great understanding, but he who is quick-tempered exalts folly (Prov. 14:29).

Rest in the Lord and wait patiently for Him; do not fret because of him who prospers in his way, because of the man who carries out wicked schemes (Ps. 37:7).

Therefore, since we have so great a cloud of witnesses surrounding us, let us also lay aside every encumbrance, and the sin which so easily entangles us, and let us run with endurance the race that is set before us, fixing our eyes on Jesus, the author and perfecter of faith, who for the joy set before Him endured the cross, despising the shame, and has sat down at the right hand of the throne of God. For consider Him who has endured such hostility by sinners against Himself, so that you may not grow weary and lose heart (Heb. 12:1-3).

Patience literally means "long suffering," or to be able to continue to suffer from life's unfairness and not throw in the towel. In other words, "Hang in there!"

You say that you can't? It's too difficult? You're right. That's why it is one of the fruits of the Spirit. It takes God's power to help you hang in there. You are running a lifelong race, but fortunately you are not on your own. He is with you.

When you're struggling, turn back to the psalmist:

I waited patiently for the Lord; and He inclined to me, and heard my cry (Ps. 40:1).[1]

QUESTIONS FOR REFLECTION

Are you facing a turbulent circumstance today? If so, are you thinking about bailing out? Do you really believe this is God's solution to your problem? Why not ask God to bring you in for a safe landing?

Note
1. Tim Ritter, *Deep Down* (Wheaton, Ill.: Tyndale House Publishers, 1995), pp. 141, adapted.

68

How Do You Use Your Time?

Therefore be careful how you walk, not as unwise men, but as wise, making the most of your time, because the days are evil. So then do not be foolish, but understand what the will of the Lord is.
—EPHESIANS 5:15-17

It's trivia time! Do you know how many minutes or even seconds there are in a day? Or a week? Strange questions? Yes and no.

Our lives always seem to revolve around time in one way or another. And we tend to view time from many different perspectives. Some run their lives by a stopwatch; others use a sundial! Some have to be at an appointment 15 minutes early; others believe the event hasn't really started until they arrive—no matter what the time! Some operate according to the mod "You work first and then you play"; others reverse that phrase.

How do you view time? Better yet, how do you use your time? Some of us were raised hearing the phrase, "You're wasting time." We heard this guilt-producing stimulus so much and so often that we incorporated it into our minds and consciences and now it seems to replay automatically! Many of us are controlled by it.

Generations often clash over how people should use their time. Those who were raised in the depression of the '30s and the war years of the '40s lived in a survival mode that is much different from the way we live today. Values and long hours for the sake of survival have been replaced by new values and long hours for the sake of obtaining more material items.

But how we use our time is an issue regardless of the generation we represent. It's not *how* we make use of our time. We can be busy and still not do much. It's *what* we do with our time that has value. Paul instructs us to "[make] the *most* of your time" (Eph. 5:16).

But for some people, the biggest waste of time is...waiting. Waiting in line at the checkout stand, the movies, the airport, on the freeway, for a parking space at the mall during the After-Christmas Sale....

Wait, wait, wait. What a waste of time. Perhaps the hardest waiting of all is waiting for God. There are times when He seems to be silent. It's hard to wait for His answer when our life is falling apart.

Much of our life is spent in waiting. There are waiting rooms in hospitals, airports and train stations. People often say to us, "Why don't you sit down and wait over there?"

Do you ever get the feeling that much of life is one big waiting room?

This kind of waiting is expressed best by Sarah Doudney in the following poem:

There are days of silent sorrow
In the seasons of our life;
There are wild despairing moments,
There are hours of mental strife;
There are times of stony anguish,
When the tears refuse to fall;
But the waiting time, my brothers,
Is the hardest time of all...

We can bear the heat of conflict,
Though the sudden, crushing blow,
Beating back our gathered forces,
For a moment lay us low;
We may rise again beneath it
None the weaker for the fall;
But the waiting time, my brothers,
Is the hardest time of all.[1]

Is there a purpose or benefit in waiting? Yes. It makes us realize how much we need God. Waiting makes us more willing to receive Him. And it makes us able to handle what life throws our way. Read the words of Isaiah:

Those who hope in the Lord will renew their strength. They will soar on wings like eagles; they will run and not grow weary, they will walk and not be faint (40:31, NIV).

There is a purpose in waiting. So, if you have to wait, use your time well whether it's on the freeway or at a checkout stand or waiting for God. You could use the time to pray, memorize Scripture or even reflect on how good the Lord has been to you. Let the psalmist's words take root in you today:

Wait for the Lord; Be strong, and let your heart take courage; Yes, wait for the Lord (Ps. 27:14).

QUESTIONS FOR REFLECTION

Does God have you in a waiting room? What are you doing with your waiting time? Are you as a single waiting for the right mate or the right job opportunity? Could it be that God would like to bring you into a deeper relationship with Him while you wait? Could it be that He would like to strengthen you as you wait for His answers? Will you wait for the Lord?

Note

1. Sarah Doudney, "The Hardest Time of All" from *The Light of the World: Poems of Faith and Consolation* by Joseph Morris and St. Clair Adams (New York: George Sully and Co., 1928), p. 64.

69

How's Your Body?

I urge you therefore, brethren, by the mercies of God, to present your bodies a living and holy sacrifice, acceptable to God, which is your spiritual service of worship. And do not be conformed to this world, but be transformed by the renewing of your mind, that you may prove what the will of God is, that which is good and acceptable and perfect.

—ROMANS 12:1,2

Do you have a full-length mirror where you live? If not, use the one at the gym where you work out. (You *do* work out, don't you?) How does your body look? Is there a right amount of muscle tone, body fat and proportion? Or do you get the feeling someone slipped in one of those weird mirrors that you find in a house of mirrors at a carnival! We come in all shapes and sizes. We have very little to do with our height except to make sure that we stand up straight. Our horizontal, our width—well, that's another matter.

It's interesting to note and understand what Scripture says about our bodies. First, we don't own our bodies. They are not ours. They never were; never will be. Our bodies belong to God. We are to present them to God as a sacrifice.

When sacrifices were presented to God in the Old Testament, the animals offered had to be the best, without blemish. But ours is a living sacrifice. We are a walking, breathing sacrifice. People should be able to look at us and say, "Now, *that's* a sacrifice to God."

But will they end the statement with an exclamation point or a question mark? An exclamation point says, "You're in great shape! Wow!" A question mark says, "You're a living sacrifice? You have to be kidding!"

A cartoon I saw shows a couple of older way-out-of-shape men. One is saying to the other "I'm at the place where it's difficult to refer to my body as a temple of the Lord. It's more like a rotunda!"

Sometimes we can't do much about the shape we're in because of heredity, glandular imbalance, a disease or a crazy mixed-up metabolism. But most of us can!

What about the food you eat? Sure, when you're single it's easier to grab a Big Mac full of cattle muscle or a Taco Bell taco filled with floor sweepings or a Jack in the Box monthly surprise than it is to take the time to fix a balanced meal. But have you ever read a book on nutrition or read the fat and cholesterol content of some of the things you put into that temple?

When you and your single friends get together for a meal, is it usually pizza, fries, cokes and whatever is handy? Once in a while, okay—but continually, it's a risk.

What about (sorry to mention it) exercise? Is it regular and aerobic? (At least four times a week is necessary to improve.) You say you don't have the money or time for a gym? Many don't. That's all right. Plenty of used pieces of home equipment are available. Or you can walk the 4-miles-an-hour routine and memorize Scripture or pray while you're doing it. Many do. And if you have a dog, take the dog along. He or she will appreciate it. If you own a cat...forget it.

One other meddling question: How do you treat your body when you are in a dating relationship? The level of sexual involvement is also a reflection of our bodies as a sacrifice to the Lord. Some Christians have literally destroyed their bodies through inappropriate sexual involvement. The herpes, HIV or other diseases turned their lives in a different direction than they intended. God isn't against sex. He created it, so it makes sense that He has the right to say how it should be used.

Remember, our bodies are temples of the Holy Spirit (see 1 Cor. 6:19). They belong to God. He is saying through this scripture: "Treat well what I've given to you, for in doing so, you honor Me and you become a testimony to others about your relationship with Me."

QUESTIONS FOR REFLECTION

How are you treating your temple? Have you ever offered your body to God as a living sacrifice? If you have mistreated your temple, will you recommit it to Him today? Will you not only use the way you eat and exercise as a testimony, but will you also allow the way you use your body sexually to be a testimony of your love for Him?

70

Jealousy: A Caring Response or Insecurity?

For you shall not worship any other god, for the Lord, whose
name is Jealous, is a jealous God.

—EXODUS 34:14

You've probably heard the expression, "It's a green-headed monster." Where did that phrase originate? No one seems to know, but it's usually applied to a condition known as...jealousy.

Jealousy often occurs when a person is involved in a romantic relationship. Consider some of the following situations that could set off those feelings. See if you can identify with any of them.

You are at a social event with your romantic interest and the person spends an inordinate amount of time talking to a person of the opposite sex. Your partner keeps talking in a positive way about a former relationship that upsets you. Your partner has lunch or dinner with a former romantic interest. Your partner joins an activity or takes up a sport where he or she comes in contact with many attractive members of the opposite sex.

In a dating relationship, jealousy usually occurs when you feel threatened by the possibility that the other person is not exclusively committed to you.

So what creates jealousy? The following are reasons others have given for their jealousy:

- Some say jealous and romantic feelings go hand in hand and if there is no jealousy, the other person doesn't care.
- Some suspect their partners because they feel guilty over their own tendencies to "drift."
- Others have said they feel jealous because they don't believe they compare favorably to others. Their own self-esteem is the culprit.
- Some become jealous and suspicious when something is either wrong or lacking in the relationship that they can't identify.

- The fear of losing a partner creates an obsession to hang on and jealousy becomes a big rodent.
- Some become jealous because their partners have shown patterns of getting involved in new relationships before severing ties with the former.
- Unfortunately, some are jealous because of the mold of their own parents. The imprinting of parental examples have led to destructive patterns in their children.

What happens to a relationship when jealousy appears? This green-headed monster creates more problems than it can resolve. It becomes a self-fulfilling prophecy because the other person tires from the lack of trust. And frequently our jealousy is not because of what our partners are doing or not doing—it's simply a reflection of the insecurities in ourselves that we need to take a hard look at!

What does the Bible say about jealousy? Doesn't the Scripture say that God is a jealous God?[1]

How can God be jealous? The Hebrew word for jealousy can also be translated "zealous," which means a strong emotion expressing desire or possession of an object. We see this in Jesus' zealousness for God's house (see John 2:17).

So how is God jealous? First, He is jealous for His name. The Israelites provoked God when they worshiped others. God wants to be worshiped as God. He wants to be first in our lives. God is jealous for His people. He wants their complete devotion, not halfhearted (see 1 Cor. 10:22).

Taking God's name in vain is a misuse. God wants His name to be sanctified and kept Holy. Are you bothered when you hear the name of God or Jesus misused as profanity? It seems common today even in the entertainment field. If you are bothered, good! What do you say about it? If you're not bothered, why not? It's something to think about because God wants us to be jealous for Him!

QUESTIONS FOR REFLECTION

What are the situations that provoke jealousy in you? Who do you want to possess? Have you surrendered possession of your life to Jesus? Are you jealous for Him?

Note

1. Michael Broder, *The Art of Staying Together* (New York: Hyperion, 1993), pp. 159-162, adapted.

71

Go Ahead, Get Good and Angry

Be angry, and yet do not sin; do not let the sun
go down on your anger.
—EPHESIANS 4:26

Did you know that anger is mentioned 455 times in the Old Testament, and 375 of those times it refers to God's anger! In the New Testament six different Greek words are used for anger.

Let's think for a moment about the positive side of anger. We need to be angry. That's right, It's okay. Ephesians 4:24 says, "be angry and sin not." The word "angry" in this verse means an anger that is an abiding, settled habit of the mind and is aroused under specific conditions. In other words, we're aware of it and in control of it. There is a just occasion for this kind of anger. Reason is involved, and when reason is present, anger such as this is right. The Scriptures not only permit it, but on some occasions *demand it!* This may sound strange if we have thought for years that anger is all wrong. But the Word of God states that we *are to be angry!* Surprised?

Christians do and should get angry at the right things, such as injustice and many of the problems we see in the world around us. Righteous anger is not sinful when it is properly directed.

Righteous anger has several characteristics. First, it must be controlled—it must not be a heated or unrestrained passion. Even if the cause is legitimate and is directed at injustice, uncontrolled anger can cause great error in judgment and increase the difficulty. *Be angry and sin not.*

Second, the anger must be void of hatred, malice or resentment. Anger that harbors a counterattack only complicates the problem. Jesus' reactions to the injustices delivered against Him are a good example of a man in control of His anger:

When He was reviled and insulted, He did not revile or offer insult in return; [when] He was abused and suffered, He made no threats [of vengeance]; but He trusted [Himself and everything] to Him Who judges fairly (1 Pet. 2:23, *Amp.*)

A third characteristic of righteous anger is that its motivation is unselfish. When the motivation for anger is selfish, usually pride and resentment are involved. Anger should be directed not at the wrong done to oneself, but at injustice done to others.

Keep in mind that anger can be used for either good or bad. Unfortunately, it's often used in a negative way, especially in families. Read through the Old Testament.

Saul's anger toward David and Jonathan is an illustration of the destructive force of anger:

And the women responded as they laughed and frolicked, saying, Saul has slain his thousands, and David his ten thousands. And Saul was very angry, for the saying displeased him (1 Sam. 18:7,8, *Amp.*).

Jealousy and envy toward David progressed to anger and hatred, which led to action—attempts to take David's life. Later Saul's anger turned toward his own son:

Then Saul's anger was kindled against Jonathan and he said to him, You son of a perverse, rebellious woman, do not I know that you have chosen the son of Jesse to your own shame and to the shame of your mother who bore you?...But Saul cast his spear at him to smite him, by which Jonathan knew that his father had determined to kill David (1 Sam. 20:30,33, *Amp.*).

When you allow yourself to be governed by emotion instead of righteousness, you may react impulsively in ways that are decidedly destructive. Each year in the United States thousands of children are abused physically because a parent's anger got out of control. Many parents and spouses live with overwhelming regrets because of actions made in anger toward other family members. Perhaps you've been on the receiving end of anger and you know the results.

So, when you are angry, take the four-step approach:

1. Delay. Put Proverbs into practice.
2. Discover the cause. It's usually fear, hurt or frustration (see Prov. 19:11, *Amp.*).
3. Say what you're feeling in a calm voice.
4. Let the person know what you want. It works. Really, it does.

What are some of the things that make you angry? What do you fear losing? What is the hurt or frustration that provokes you? Have you ever been righteously angry? What is the difference between that kind of anger and the anger that causes you to lash out at others?

72

You're a Creature of Habit

Knowing this, that our old self was crucified with Him,
that our body of sin might be done away with, that we
should no longer be slaves to sin.
—ROMANS 6:6

The alarm goes off with a shrill ring. Your hand reaches out and without thinking you hit the "off" button. With half-opened eyes, you climb out of bed and head toward the bathroom. On the way, you slip your feet into slippers, grab a robe with your left hand and swing your right hand and arm into the sleeve. Then you walk into the bathroom and shut the door. With your left hand you grab the toothbrush—with your right, you grab the toothpaste—all in one easy motion.

After the bathroom, you walk into the kitchen and nod to the dog. Your left hand automatically flips on the coffeemaker, which was stocked the night before. Your right hand opens the refrigerator and grabs the orange juice. The next 20 minutes are a carbon copy of the more than 168 small but important behaviors that get you ready to face the hard, cruel world.

Did you think about each behavior? Did you have to talk yourself into doing this and then doing that? Of course not! These actions just came naturally to you. You were programmed. As you did each little act year after year, they became automatic. In fact, each morning when you arise, you shift into automatic and begin to function. Do you know what these automatic actions are called? Habits! You have trained yourself well.

We need to develop some habits, especially those that help us get through the day. Some habits are beneficial; some are crippling. We tend to have both.

You're a creature of habit. You may not like to hear that and prefer thinking you're flexible. But most of what you think, say or do comes from habits you have developed. Habits are always in operation whether you are aware of them or not. What you've learned, you tend to practice and this is what you become.

As much as 98 percent of what you do is the result of habit rather than choice. Habits operate outside the conscious mind whereas choice is in the conscious mind.

Whatever you do again and again becomes a habit. What you practice, you also become good at.

Are you aware of what it takes to change a habit? Did you know that to make even a small positive behavior a part of your repertoire of behaviors will take at least 18 repetitions over a period of 18 days?

But negative habits are not what the Scriptures encourage us to practice! I've had people share that with me.

Every living thing will fight to the death to stay alive. So too, habits are living things. Expect resistance.

Take a look at your habits. Which of them reflect the presence of Jesus in your life?

QUESTIONS FOR REFLECTION

What are some of your daily habits? Are you even aware of which shoe you put on first? What do your habits say about you? Which of your habits would you like to eliminate? What habits would you like to incorporate into your daily life? Are you willing to let God help you change your habits? When will you begin?

73

Yes, You Can Change

Therefore if any man is in Christ, he is a new creature; the old things passed away; behold, new things have come.

—2 CORINTHIANS 5:17

Do you *really* want to change some of your habits? It is possible. But you'll have to start with changing your mind. After all, your mind is where your words, your behaviors and many of your emotional responses begin.

We all came into life with a mind that has been affected by the fall of man. We begin life with a mind that has a propensity toward negative thinking, worry, fear, guilt and remembering experiences that would be better off relinquished. Even when we become believers, the residue of old thinking is still with us.

This unhealthy thinking brings its influence into play with our wills, our emotions, our thoughts and our behaviors. And relationships are the playground where these tendencies can romp. That's why some begin a relationship, then break it off, start over and...well, you know the pattern.

The healing of some conflicts and destructive patterns is difficult because of the defenses we have built around ourselves to keep from directly confronting our responsibilities.

But the presence of Christ in our lives empowers us to be different. He gives us two possibilities for growth. First, He changes the old patterns by eliminating the effects of prior hurts in our lives. Second, He helps us use our minds, emotions and wills to behave in new, more positive ways, both now and in the future.

Our task then, through Christ, is to remove the rough edges that drain our energies and keep us from moving forward. And it begins in our minds. The Scriptures are clear about this. The Bible tells us that as a man thinks so is he (see Prov. 23:7). Paul tells us we need a spiritual mind (see Rom. 8:6), a renewed mind (see Eph. 4:23), a transformed mind (see Rom. 12:2), a Christlike mind (see 1 Cor. 2:11) and a sound mind (see 2 Tim. 1:7). If you want both joy in your life and the possibility of change in your life, the answer is transformed thinking.

There is also a *second element* involved in change that you may not be expecting. It's called *praise*. Praise for what God has done, for who He is and what He will do releases to Him the tight control we've had on our lives.

It's easy to praise God for what He has done, because we can reflect back and measure the actual results. We have something tangible, and there is little risk involved.

But what do you expect in the future for you and for your relationships? Is it difficult for you to praise God for what He is going to do? Praise opens your life to some possibilities you may have never considered. By praising God, you not only become a risk taker and a change maker, but you become more aware of what God wants for you. This may be an uncomfortable idea for you. It may mean that you praise God in an unpleasant circumstance. It may mean praising God in spite of that taxing personal relationship you've had for several years.

Dr. Lloyd Ogilvie has an interesting thought along this line:

Consistent praise over a period of time conditions us to receive what the Lord has been waiting patiently to reveal to us or release for us.[1]

When you and I rejoice in the Lord, we don't do it because we feel like it. It is an act of our wills, a commitment. When we rejoice in the Lord, we begin to see life from another point of view.

You may be thinking that you're too busy during the day to stop and praise God. That's just the time you need to do it—when you are too busy, fretful and overwhelmed. When your mind is cluttered with concerns about your life, stop...clear your mind and praise God. You'll feel refreshed.

Praising God in advance of a solution is an act of faith, a way of saying, "I don't know the outcome, but I am willing to trust."

Can you think of a better way?

QUESTIONS FOR REFLECTION

In what ways do you need to transform your thinking? What are some of the old thinking patterns that keep you in bondage to your past? Have you thought about praising God in the midst of your frustrations, temptations and overwhelming difficulties? Who or what do you put your trust in when you don't know the outcome?

Note

1. Lloyd John Ogilvie, *God's Will in My Life* (Eugene, Oreg.: Harvest House, 1982), p. 136.

74

Would You Like to Be Wealthy?

A rich man's wealth is his strong city.
—PROVERBS 18:11

Would you like to be wealthy? What a ridiculous question! Who wouldn't? Most of us think that wealth will solve all our problems. When we are single, we often believe it will attract the right person to us or provide a lifestyle that is free from any responsibility. Perhaps. Wealth will provide security. And that's what everyone wants. Proverbs affirms this when it says that "the rich man's wealth is his fortress, the ruin of the poor is their poverty" (10:15).

If you have a large savings account, trust fund and multiple IRA's, you feel like the writer of Proverbs—you have a fortress. But look at the complete passage in Proverbs 18:11:

A rich man's wealth is his strong city, and like a high wall in his own imagination.

According to this passage, the rich only imagine they are secure. Their security is only in their dreams. The security of wealth is limited:

He who trusts in his riches will fall, but the righteous will flourish like the green leaf (11:28).

Wealth buys friends, doesn't it? Sure. We're attracted to wealthy people because we live vicariously through what they have. The book of Proverbs affirms this when it says that "the poor is hated even by his neighbor, but those who love the rich are many" (14:20). It seems that money does buy friends, but are they really friends? Would these so-called friends remain faithful if the wealthy suddenly became poor?

Wealth does more than buy friends, it also ransoms our lives: "The ransom of a man's life is his riches, but the poor hears no rebuke" (13:8). The wealthier you are, the more of a target you are—not just for ransom, but for others hitting you up for something.

We need to remember that when our economy collapses, and it will, all the wealth in the world won't get us out of that mess: "Riches do not profit in the day of wrath, but righteousness delivers from death" (11:4).

More wealth does buy power in this world: "The rich rules over the poor, and the borrower becomes the lender's slave" (22:7).

But there is another major problem with being wealthy. Your wealth can go to your head. Your money can become your identity, but there is no depth or substance to that identity. "The rich man is wise in his own eyes, but the poor who has understanding sees through him" (28:11). "There is one who pretends to be rich, but has nothing; another pretends to be poor, but has great wealth" (13:7).

Do you still want to be wealthy? Perhaps. Especially when you hear about the ridiculous amounts athletes or movie celebrities are paid. But who do they become from all that fame and fortune?

Before you press on to a life of trying to be rich, you may want to consider something else Proverbs has to say. It's really quite simple: It's better to be a person of integrity than to be wealthy: "Better is the poor who walks in his integrity, than he who is crooked though he be rich" (28:6). "Better is a poor man who walks in his integrity than he who is perverse in speech and is a fool" (19:1). "Better is a little with righteousness than great income with injustice" (16:8).

It's better to have reverence for God than to be wealthy and have the trouble wealth can bring when He is not a part of it: "Better is a little with the fear of the Lord, than great treasure and turmoil with it" (15:16).

Finally, it's actually better to live a life of moderation than to be wealthy: "Two things I asked of Thee, do not refuse me before I die; keep deception and lies far from me, give me neither poverty nor riches; feed me with the food that is my portion, lest I be full and deny Thee and say, 'Who is the Lord?' Or lest I be in want and steal, and profane the name of my God" (30:7-9).

So, if you still want to strive to be wealthy, go ahead. But you don't have to. You're already wealthy if you know Jesus. The riches you have in Christ are far better than anything the world has to offer.[1]

What are some of the lies that you have believed about wealth? Have you found your identity in something you own rather than who you are in Christ? If so, which of today's verses do you need to apply to your life to have the riches that make you rich in God's eyes?

Note

1. Robert Hicks, *In Search of Wisdom* (Colorado Springs: NavPress, 1995), pp. 92-101, adapted.

You'd Be Amazed
What Gentleness
Can Do

But the fruit of the Spirit is...gentleness.
—GALATIANS 5:22,23

If you want to get ahead in life, be assertive, overbearing and violent if necessary. That's the way some people live life. But it's not the way to build loving relationships, nor is it the way to show that God's Spirit is at work within you.

If you want to stand out, be noticed and be remembered—be gentle. Have you heard expressions such as, "That person has such a gentle touch"; "He has such a gentle way about him"; or "Wasn't that a gentle landing? You couldn't even feel the wheels of that 747 touching the landing strip!"?

You've probably read scriptures about being gentle. But do you really know what "gentle" means? The Greek word is also translated "meekness" or "humility." Pastor Tim Ritter describes it in this way:

Gentleness expresses itself in: "God-given strength to control our attitudes and actions so we can deal with people according to their needs, not according to our own weakness."

Gentleness is a character trait that demonstrates a mild disposition and temperate, considerate spirit. Gentleness chooses the best way to respond, without automatically becoming angry, harsh or violent.

Gentleness is strength under control. Sometimes gentleness demonstrates itself with firmness and power, but that's a godly choice, not a natural reaction.

Gentleness includes humility and refusal to place our desires above others.

Our society places a low value on gentleness as a character trait because people want power, strength and assertiveness. But God has a different perspective.[1]

Gentleness is a quality that God values greatly. Listen to His Words from the Psalms:

But the humble will inherit the land, and will delight themselves in abundant prosperity (37:11).

And in Thy majesty ride on victoriously, for the cause of truth and meekness and righteousness; let Thy right hand teach Thee awesome things (45:4).

For the Lord takes pleasure in His people; He will beautify the afflicted ones with salvation (149:4).

One of the most significant descriptions of Jesus, the one who created the universes, the Son of God, is from the book of Isaiah. It is a description of power and control:

Behold, My Servant, whom I uphold; My chosen one in whom My soul delights. I have put My Spirit upon Him; He will bring forth justice to the nations. He will not cry out or raise His voice, nor make His voice heard in the street. A bruised reed He will not break, and a dimly burning wick He will not extinguish; He will faithfully bring forth justice. He will not be disheartened or crushed, until He has established justice in the earth; and the coastlands will wait expectantly for His law (42:1-4).

He wants us to live our lives being gentle. But what will gentleness really do for us? Good question. After all, there's got to be some benefit in all of this. You will discover when gentleness becomes part of your life that you handle conflict in a much healthier way and move more quickly toward resolution. God's Word tells us that the best way to deal with problems is in a gentle manner:

But refuse foolish and ignorant speculations, knowing that they produce quarrels. And the Lord's bond-servant must not be quarrelsome, but be kind to all, able to teach, patient when wronged, with gentleness correcting those who are in opposition, if perhaps God may grant them repentance leading to the knowledge of the truth (2 Tim. 2:23-25).

When you're threatened and fearful of others being overbearing and controlling you, a persistent gentle approach will help you stand firm and end up being in control:

A gentle answer turns away wrath, but a harsh word stirs up anger (Prov. 15:1).

It's difficult for gentleness to exist with selfishness. People are repelled by those who are selfish, but drawn to people with a gentle spirit:

But you, man of God, flee from all this, and pursue righteousness, godliness, faith, love, endurance and gentleness (1 Tim. 6:11, *NIV*).

Some of the most respected leaders in the world have been those described with the words *gentle, humble* and *meek.*

It may not be easy to live this way. We are all self-protective. But we can choose to live this way and develop this character trait. God must think we need it. If not, why all the scriptural teaching about it?

It's something to think about.[2]

QUESTIONS FOR REFLECTION

Are you a gentle person? How do you respond to those who hurt you deeply? Do you deal with people according to their needs or your own weakness? When you must act firmly, is it a controlled act of righteousness or a reaction of your will? Who do you need to be more gentle with? What steps are you willing to take to develop this admirable character trait?

Notes
1. Tim Ritter, *Deep Down* (Wheaton, Ill.: Tyndale House Publishers, 1995), p. 141.
2. Ibid., pp. 141-149, adapted.

76

All Work and No Play

Six days you shall labor and do all your work.
—EXODUS 20:9

Are you a workaholic? You know, that person who is a blur as he rushes by, talking on the phone, checking his or her watch and grabbing something to eat while running to catch a cab. Hustle and hurry (hurry? can't read this word) are the key words in his life. Workaholism is a trap many of us fall into. It's also a trap we can escape.

When you are single and on the way up in your profession, it's easy to fall into the pattern of work, more work and nothing but work. This all-work-and-no-play pattern can happen whether you are struggling to barely pay the bills or trying to accumulate as much as you can while you can. One of the by-products of this lifestyle is the little time it leaves to cultivate pleasurable relationships.

Perhaps you are a workaholic and don't know it. Or someone you know is. Maybe that someone is a friend, parent or a person you are interested in for a relationship. Workaholism can subtly creep into all of our lives without our awareness.

It happens to men and women of all ages. In some businesses and companies, nonstop work is the only way to get ahead, to climb the ladder of success.

Workaholics work hard, but not all hard workers are workaholics. Hard workers work to gain a promotion, to earn more money or to please someone. Workaholism differs in its approach or attitude toward work. Workaholics think about work when they are not working. **They love working!** They can't get enough. They go out to dinner with friends or sit in church, but their minds are always at work.

They can be found in every class of society, gender and occupation, and they all have the same passion—work. Many of them are very happy. The problem is that those around them are often unhappy. Workaholics are rarely at home, and when they are, they don't participate much. Some workaholics use their homes just for sleeping, and it looks like it too!

If you are a workaholic, what are you really like? Do you want to know? Let's assume you have this tendency and take a look at your profile:

Several standard characteristics fit all workaholics. You're intense, energetic, competitive and driven. You enjoy what you do. You wake up in the morning and can't wait to get started. You drive yourself and compete with others. Often you compare with others the number of hours per week that you work.

You probably also have strong self-doubts. Others would not suspect this by looking at you because you cover it well. You suspect that you are inadequate, so you work hard to compensate. You believe: "The workaholics trade sweat for talent." You think the way to overcome these feelings of inadequacy is to do more.

If you're a dyed-in-the-wool workaholic, you prefer work to leisure. There is no holiday or work separation, it all blurs together. Your home or apartment may be a branch office or extension of your profession. Saving time is a goal. You glance at your watch frequently. You sleep less, and meals are functional (in other words, mealtimes are for eating, not socializing). You make schedules well in advance, punch the walk button several times at street corners and plan, plan, plan.

Does it wear you out to read this description? How does workaholism fit in relationships, friendships, church, prayer, and...waiting on the Lord? It doesn't. Is workaholism a spiritual calling? No.

But there is a better way to live. It's called balance. It happens when you make a choice to enjoy life, enjoy yourself and others, and enjoy God.

You may have decided after reading this, it's not you! If so, rejoice. But what if this workaholic profile is your boss and he or she wants you to adapt this lifestyle? What if it's a potential spouse? Would you like to live with a person like this? What would happen to you if you did? Don't let others force you into this lifestyle. Watch for the warning signs: all work and no play. Pray for yourself and those you see falling into this trap.

Read the book, *The Rhythm of Life* by Richard Exley, (Honor Books). It could impact your life, and remember: It's called balance—enjoying life; enjoying yourself; and enjoying God.

QUESTIONS FOR REFLECTION

Is your life filled with all work and no play? Do you fit the workaholic profile? What does God call this lifestyle? Who and what are you living for? What do you fear would happen if you lowered your standard of living to make room for some pleasure? If you are dating a workaholic, why?

77

How Do You Communicate?

The tongue of the wise makes knowledge acceptable, but the mouth of fools spouts folly.

—PROVERBS 15:2

Communication is to a relationship what blood is to the body. Strong statement? Yes, but relationships die when there's no communication just as the body does without that all-important substance—blood.

Perhaps you've been in a relationship in which the other person had very little ability to communicate. You know...they either didn't say anything, gave you one-or-two-word responses or gave frustrating "I don't know" replies to your questions! Communication such as this can drive you up a wall!

Communication is one of the most frequently mentioned problems in all types of relationships whether they be at work, in families of origin or with potentially hopeful relationships. Scores of books have been written about this subject, but there is only one book and always will be that surpasses the others in dealing with communication—the book of Proverbs.

Here's a trivia question for you: How many times are the words *tongue, mouth, lips and words* mentioned in Proverbs? The answer is coming later; but suffice it to say, this book is the finest guide we have ever had for learning how to communicate. And in practical advice, it surpasses all the other books in the Bible. Consider then the following advice on what *not* to say. You may find what it says surprising about...

- Boasting: "Like clouds and wind without rain is a man who boasts of gifts he does not give" (Prov. 25:14, *NIV*). This is the kind of talking that is useless, ridiculous and even profane. Paul admonishes us: "Do not let any unwholesome talk come out of your mouths, but only what is helpful for building others up...that it may benefit those who listen" (Eph. 4:29, *NIV*). As you look at your communication pattern, is it far from calling attention to yourself? Remember, boasting lets others know you're insecure.

- Flattery: "He who rebukes a man will in the end gain more favor than he who has a flattering tongue" (Prov. 28:23, *NIV*). We know how to butter up someone, especially when we want something. Flattery is all about using insincere compliments to deceive someone. It's a method to get what we want by manipulation.

- Being verbose and running off at the mouth: Look at Proverbs 10:19 in *The Living Bible*: "Don't talk so much. You keep putting your foot in your mouth. Be sensible and turn off the flow!" That's graphic! You've met people like this. They fill the air with words—empty words of no significance. They don't know the meaning of listening. It's as though they enjoy hearing themselves talk and lack the social sensitivity to know that no one else really cares what they are saying. Have you ever put on a tape recorder to catch a conversation? Try it sometime. It's a real learning experience!

- Angry, argumentative words: "An angry man stirs up dissension, and a hot-tempered one commits many sins" (Prov. 29:22, *NIV*). Strife implies rigidity, stubbornness and unhealthy anger. Purposeful, constructive, resolvable arguments are healthy. But many arguments are not conducted in this spirit.

If you would like to read some other powerful passages in Proverbs about communication and anger, begin with Proverbs 14:16,17; 15:4; 17:14,22,24,25. And those are just for starters. As you read, which verses do you think would strengthen your life if you applied them?

By the way, the answer to my trivia question is "more than 150"! Why not take a highlighter, read through Proverbs and identify each one. Then, work on applying them to your life!

QUESTIONS FOR REFLECTION

Do you drive others up a wall with your verbose communication or lack of it? Do you boast? Do you flatter others to get what you want? Are you argumentative? Do you believe God wants you to be a better communicator? If so, are you willing to obey the guidelines He has laid out for you in Proverbs? When will you start?

78

What Kind of a Friend Are You?

*Now it came about when he had finished speaking to Saul,
that the soul of Jonathan was knit to the soul of David, and
Jonathan loved him as himself.*

—1 SAMUEL 18:1

Friendship—we were created for it. If you have some close friends, you are rich. We all need them. Friends help to complete our lives. And here's something else you may not be aware of: Romantic relationships that evolve out of friendship form the best basis for lasting marriage. God's Word has much to say about friendship.

If ever two men had a close friendship, it was David and Jonathan. In fact, they are a great model for what it means to have a close friendship.

Real friendship is deeper than acquaintances (those we work with, workout with or share a mutual fence with). Real friendship means to be one in spirit.

"One in spirit" means you are on the same wavelength. You connect, you relate well, you share similar values and a similar view of life. When you're both Christians, you know the same God and want the same things for your lives.

Let's look further into the friendship of David and Jonathan in 1 Samuel 18. There was an intense bonding of love: "And Jonathan loved him [David] as himself" (v. 1).

Friendship involves a deep commitment to the other person and a willingness to be vulnerable. We see this in verses three and four: "And Jonathan made a covenant with David because he loved him as himself. Jonathan took off the robe he was wearing and gave it to David, along with his tunic, and even his sword, his bow and his belt" (vv. 3,4, *NIV*).

Friendship involves loyalty—sticking to the other person during times of difficulty. Jonathan's father Saul wanted to kill David, but "Jonathan spoke well of David" (1 Sam. 19:4, *NIV*). True friends speak well of one another when they're not together. They focus on the positive and let the negatives slide.

Close friends encourage each other. When David was discouraged and hiding from those who wanted to hurt him, Jonathan came through: "And Saul's son Jonathan went to David at Horesh and helped him find strength in God" (1 Sam. 23:16, *NIV*).

The examples of David and Jonathan provide a great prototype for friendship. But are you also aware of what Proverbs says about friendship? Proverbs is emphatic that a few close friends are better than a lot of acquaintances. One characteristic that is greatly emphasized in Proverbs is reflected in the relationship of David and Jonathan—consistency. Real friends stick to you no matter what:

A friend loves at all times, and a brother is born for adversity (17:17).

This is the kind of friendship you are urged to give:

Do not forsake your own friend or your father's friend, and do not go to your brother's house in the day of your calamity; better is a neighbor who is near than a brother far away (27:10).

Another characteristic highlighted in Proverbs is candor. Friends can tell it like it is:

A man who flatters his neighbor is spreading a net for his steps (29:5).

Candor builds rather than tears down the friendship. Directness adds to the relationship rather than distracts.

One of the advantages of friendship is the two-way counsel or help that can occur. Some of the counsel has the effect of cheering you on and some may challenge you, but a true friendship has both elements:

Oil and perfume make the heart glad, so a man's counsel is sweet to his friend (27:9).

Iron sharpens iron, so one man sharpens another (27:17).

Another characteristic is something often lacking today—tact. Respect for another person's feelings—not being intrusive—is a reflection of tact:

He who blesses his friend with a loud voice early in the morning, it will be reckoned a curse to him (27:14).

Like a madman who throws firebrands, arrows and death, so is the man who deceives his neighbor, and says, "Was I not joking?" (26:18,19).

So, the big question is not, Do your friends reflect these qualities? The question is, Do you? When you are a loyal friend to others, others will want to be a loyal friend to you.

QUESTIONS FOR REFLECTION

Do you value your friendships? What are the qualities that make you a good friend to others? As you read the scriptures for today, what were some of the weaknesses you discovered in yourself? What steps are you willing to take to be a better friend?

79

Get Rid of
Excess Baggage

Brethren, I do not regard myself as having laid hold of it
yet; but one thing I do: forgetting what lies behind and
reaching forward to what lies ahead.
—PHILIPPIANS 3:13

When you travel on an airline, it's not uncommon to discover that you have excess baggage. The problem is that you are only allowed to check through so many bags. You can check in the excess, but it will cost you. It used to cost $10 a bag, then $20—now the charge is $50!

Many of us are going through life with some excess baggage and it's costing us. It's also robbing us...of joy, of being productive and of achieving our potential.

We pack our excess baggage with numerous items. Some of us fill it with hurts we carry around from the past—maybe an embarrassing incident in adolescence that keeps us from experiencing life to the fullest. It could be abuse from a parent or other relative. It might be the hurt of a broken relationship or the betrayal of trust in a friendship. But it still hurts. There's another kind of baggage we carry, too.

Some of us carry baggage from giving in to peer pressure when we were younger. We liked the results so much that traveling this way became a way of life—even into adulthood. We compromise our beliefs and values for the momentary approval of those around us, and usually discover we are not really in charge of our lives at all. Others are.

Let me use my "meddle" detector to really dig through the excess baggage. I'm looking for something a lot of people carry that is often evident to others. It's a little three-letter word called "ego." Ego is nothing more than an inflated, distorted sense of importance. You've seen it in others. People with this extra baggage introduce themselves by their titles, their diplomas, by what they drive and what they've accomplished. They want you to identify them by what they've accomplished or accumulated rather than getting to know them for who they are. They want others to think they are unique or special so they tell them why they are. Usually, however, what they have to tell produces the opposite effect. Do you know anyone who's packed a little too much ego?

With all the baggage some people carry, they eventually begin to feel like pack animals. For years pack animals have been used to carry the excess baggage. If you've ever been backpacking on a hunting or fishing trip into the high country, you're glad to have those mules or burros along to carry all the gear. And if you're fortunate, you've got a guide along who knows how to load and unload the animals. It's a lot of work and to add to the work, sometimes the animals are in foul moods. These stubborn creatures either kick you or try to take a bite out of you!

In the Far East, camels are the mainstay for the desert traveler. And in Jesus' day they were very common. His statement in this verse has more significance to it than meets the eye:

> Again I say to you, it is easier for a camel to go through the eye of a needle, than for a rich man to enter the kingdom of God (Matt. 19:24).

One of the gates in the Old Jerusalem wall was actually called the Needle's Eye Gate. It was very narrow, just barely wide enough for a camel. The problem was the baggage. It wouldn't fit. The merchants had to downsize their camels. They had to unload them, walk them through the gate, bring the baggage through and, if they had farther to go, reload the beasts. Only when a camel was unloaded could it get through the gate. It had to get rid of its baggage.

Jesus said, "Enter through the narrow gate. For wide is the gate and broad is the road that leads to destruction, and many enter through it" (Matt. 7:13, *NIV*).

What about it? Are you carrying any baggage or burdens that make it difficult for you to enter the narrow gate? Just as with the camel, something may need to be stripped off. Take a look at your load. Something may need to be unloaded before you can get through.[1]

QUESTIONS FOR REFLECTION

What kinds of excess baggage are you carrying today? Have you been dragging around childhood hurts and attitudes that keep your life from taking off? Perhaps you are flying high on an ego that needs to be deflated. Are you ready for your reality check? What excess baggage would you have to unload to pass through the Eye of the Needle today?

Note
1. Judson Edwards, *Regaining Control of Your Life* (Minneapolis: Bethany, 1989), p. 157, adapted.

80

What's Your Weakness?

I am speaking in human terms because of the weakness of your flesh. For just as you presented your members as slaves to impurity and to lawlessness, resulting in further lawlessness, so now present your members as slaves to righteousness, resulting in sanctification.

—ROMANS 6:19

It's embarrassing. Someone asks you to open a jar, you take it and try for all you're worth, but you can't do it. Then some little kid comes along who knows how to put the right amount of pressure to it and snap! It opens. You're at the gym pumping iron (translation: attempting to lift weights) and you grab the bar, get your muscles ready and then...nothing. The weights stay on the floor. Somebody glued them there! No, just like the lid on the jar, you weren't strong enough. You were too weak! What's new about that?

We're all weak. We've all got our Achilles' heel that we don't like to admit to. We try to compensate for our physical weaknesses by working out hour after hour in health clubs and going to health food stores for vitamin supplements. Even with all the time we spend in preparation to develop defenses and to build walls of resistance, something always surfaces to bring us to our knees.

In a way we're similar to Superman. Remember him? He's been around in comics, films and TV for years. He even got married in a TV series in 1996! The man of steel was faster than a locomotive and could leap tall buildings in a single bound. Nothing but nothing could stop him—except kryptonite. It was a substance from his home planet. It could not only weaken him, it could kill him with prolonged exposure. Perhaps you too remember the scenes when he tried to leap or run or fly but couldn't because of exposure to kryptonite. He was weakened.

If even Superman had a weakness, is there any hope for us? There are many varieties of kryptonite out there. Some of it is attractive, too: more money, bigger houses, BMWs, popularity with glances from attractive people and more.

As Christians we may have set standards based upon God's Word for what we say, how we treat others, not working on Sundays, watching what we eat or drink, but then the pressure comes. All of a sudden we cave in. Our standards didn't stand up—we weakened. We all have our weaknesses. What's yours?

When you admit it, face it, confess it and ask Jesus Christ to help you with it, that weakness loses its power. And that weak area of your life begins to diminish. Sharing your weakness with a trusted friend can also help to develop a two-way accountability.

There is a state of weakness that is positive, though. This happens when we acknowledge that we really are insufficient and weak in the flesh so we lean upon the suffering of Christ in order that real strength will come. The apostle Paul learned to live in this positive state of weakness:

> But he said to me, *"My grace is sufficient for you, for my power is made perfect in weakness."* Therefore I will boast all the more gladly about my weaknesses, so that Christ's power may rest on me. That is why, for Christ's sake, I delight in weaknesses, in insults, in hardships, in persecutions, in difficulties. For when I am weak, then I am strong (2 Cor. 12:9,10, *NIV*, italics added).

It's all right to be weak. There's a strength in being weak. Let Jesus work through you to give you a strength you never dreamed possible!

QUESTIONS FOR REFLECTION

Where are you weak? How much power does this weakness have over you? Have you confessed it to God and one other trusted person? Have you found God's strength in this weakness yet? If not, what prevents you from surrendering this area of your life to Him? Will you allow Him to love you and care for you in your weakness?

81

How's Your Appetite?

But He answered and said, "It is written, 'Man shall
not live on bread alone, but on every word that proceeds
out of the mouth of God.'"
—MATTHEW 4:4

The aroma captivates your senses. It's your favorite food and you haven't eaten for hours. You hear your stomach rumble as the pangs of hunger hit. Your mouth begins to salivate at the thought of just one taste. Eating! Much of our lives centers around where to eat, what to eat and when to eat. We plan our days, our outings, our business deals and even our lives around eating. Some eat to live. Others live to eat! It seems like such a basic simple process.

But eating can be misused. It's become an addictive habit for some. Others choose to eat the wrong foods even though their cholesterol hovers around 300! Sometimes the way we eat becomes a window so others can see the inner problems we have, especially when we have an eating disorder.

A whole range of eating disorders has emerged in our culture: overeating, eating the wrong stuff, undereating, not eating, anorexia, bulimia and more. They all have their own set of problems. We tend to think eating disorders are only a modern-day problem. But we first read about them in Proverbs:

Do not associate with winebibbers; be not among them nor among gluttonous eaters of meat, for the drunkard and the glutton shall come to poverty, and drowsiness shall clothe a man with rags" (Prov. 23:20,21, *Amp.*).

It's sad to see pictures of anorexics who literally destroy their bodies and sometimes their lives by starving themselves. Sometimes the people we admire in the world of entertainment or athletics with the "perfect" shapes maintain themselves by being bulimic. They're held captive by their desire to be perfect.

Usually we think of eating disorders associated with women, but men engage in anorexia and bulimia just as women do.

There are others we call diet freaks whose entire lives are dictated by this diet or that. But there are many who manifest eating disorders in a different way—spiritually!

Anorexia is body emaciation caused by a physical aversion to food and eating. Bulimia is the binge-and-purge disorder. But listen to how these two disorders have been described in the spiritual realm:

Spiritual anorexia is an aversion to feeding from the Word of God. It is impossible for anyone to stand and fight in spiritual warfare if he or she is spiritually malnourished. This is why the enemy will do whatever is necessary to keep us from reading and meditating on the Scriptures. Jesus put it this way in His dialogue with Satan: "Man shall not live by bread alone, but on every word that proceeds out of the mouth of God" (Matt. 4:4).

If you are not consistently taking in the Scriptures, then you will become weak, sickly and easily overcome by temptation. You may believe in the Bible and believe that it is God's Word, but if you are not feeding from the Bible, you are easy prey for the enemy. That's why the enemy attempts to disrupt the appointments you make to meet with the Lord in prayer and in His Word.

As dangerous as spiritual anorexia is, there's another disorder that is even more dangerous. Watch out for this one! Bulimia is an eating disorder that is commonly known as the binge-and-purge syndrome. You know, you eat as much as you want to the point of overeating. And then (this is the gross part!) you regurgitate or take an overdose of laxatives to get rid of food.

Spiritual bulimia is knowing the Word of God without *doing* it. Or as James described, it is *hearing* the Word of God without doing it. Spiritual bulimia is characteristic of those who binge on truth—through books, tapes, good Bible teaching or listening to a favorite communicator on the radio. You take in and in and in, but nothing happens. That's why the spiritual bulimic appears to be so righteous. There's just one problem. The bulimic knows the truth, but doesn't apply it.[1]

When you are undernourished physically, the answer is to eat and digest food. When you are undernourished spiritually, the answer is to eat, digest more of the Word and then apply it so your life is different.[2]

QUESTIONS FOR REFLECTION

Do you have a spiritual eating disorder? Do you eat at least one spiritual meal a day? If not, what changes do you need to make in your schedule to keep from spiritually starving to death? Are you eating

*without processing your spiritual meals? What changes do you
need to make to become a person who turns the food into action
or energy through application?*

Notes

1. Bill McCartney, ed., *What Makes A Man* (Colorado Springs: NavPress, 1992). From an article by Steve Farrar, 58-59, adapted.
2. H. Norman Wright, *With All My Strength* (Ann Arbor, Mich.: Servant Publications, 1996), January 21, adapted.

82

One-Sided Relationships

And be subject to one another in the fear of Christ.
—EPHESIANS 5:21

When you're single and wanting to build a close relationship that may become permanent, you have certain dreams, hopes and expectations. Everyone does. That's quite normal. In fact you need to if you're thinking of spending the rest of your life with this person.

One of your expectations is that he or she will contribute to the relationship as much as you will. It will take two of you giving to each other to make it work. A husband who had been married for more than 25 years remarked, "Marriage is not a 50-50 proposition, as is so often said: It's more of a 90-10 relationship. Sometimes you give 90 percent and sometimes you receive 10 percent, but don't ever attempt to keep score!" Excellent advice.

But sometimes you find after being in a relationship for a while that something just isn't right. At first you can't put your finger on it. Then it becomes apparent that it's a one-sided relationship. You discover a pattern of inequity!

Let's look at some of the signs to be aware of in any relationship:

You seem to be the one who is always giving. The other person takes and takes but doesn't seem to be aware of your needs or doesn't care to meet them. Can't you just imagine being married to someone like that!? You end up feeling enslaved. It's not a very biblical pattern for any relationship—it's one-sided.

Another indicator of a one-sided relationship is being with someone who refuses to allow you to break off the relationship. The person holds you for "emotional ransom" by threatening you with what will happen if you do end it. It could be suicide, spreading rumors about you or any other dire consequence that can be hurled at you. Thus you remain stuck. But why would anyone want to stay with a person so insecure and troubled? Unfortunately, some do and usually because they believe they will be able to help straighten out the other person.

You are in a one-sided relationship if your partner expects you to fulfill all of his or her needs and sees others, even same-sex friends, as threatening to your relationship. You feel both monopolized and restricted by being in the relationship.

You are in a one-way relationship if you live in fear from constant threats by the other person to leave if a difference or disagreement arises. Much of your time is spent making sure you don't make any waves. You eventually feel as though you are walking around on eggshells.

If your partner is causing the erosion of your own sense of adequacy and self-esteem, you are not only in a one-way, but an unhealthy relationship.

It could also be that you are devoting much of your time to building up his or her sense of self-worth to the exclusion of your own life goals or needs for fulfillment.

One-sided relationships are very evident when your partner is narcissistic. The other person feels he or she is so unique and special that the world owes him or her. These people don't believe they have to conform as others do and they require enormous amounts of attention to the exclusion of your own needs. You struggle for anything you receive. It's difficult to love people who are so much in love with themselves!

Perhaps one or several of these descriptions fits your relationship. Perhaps not, but it could apply to a friend. Or this could happen in the future. If so, think about this:

No matter what your efforts may be, this other person is not likely to change. You are not called to be either a reformer or a doormat in any relationship. If you have a relationship like this and you choose to stay with it, why? What does this say about your own needs of self-worth? God wants something more for you. Remember Scripture calls us to be patient, be wise and look to God for His leading.[1]

QUESTIONS FOR REFLECTION

Have you ever experienced a one-sided relationship? Are you either a reformer or a doormat? What did you hope to gain from the relationship? What signs did you overlook? Why? What would you tell a friend who is in a one-sided relationship?

Note
1. Michael S. Broder, *The Art of Staying Together* (New York: Hyperion, 1993), pp. 129-131, adapted.

83

Who Was Jesus, Really?

In these last days [He] has spoken to us in His Son,
whom He appointed heir of all things, through whom
also He made the world....Thomas answered and said to Him,
"My Lord and my God!"
—HEBREWS 1:2; JOHN 20:28

If you're a Christian, you're a follower of Jesus, right? Right. You're following someone who was a man, a flesh-and-blood person like the rest of us. That's a fact. And Jesus was also God. That too is a fact. But what would you say to a nonbeliever at work who asked you, "How can Jesus be God? I read somewhere that He was the Son of God. But who was He really?" That's a good question. Could you give an answer? Think about it.

How *can* Jesus be God? Paul wrote about Jesus: "Who, being in very nature God" (Phil. 2:6). You've probably used the word "nature" at times in reference to your child. Maybe you've said, "That's just his nature" or "He's got his father's/mother's nature." In Philippians 2:6, "nature" means Jesus is permanently identified with the nature and character of God. His divinity has always been there and comes from within Him.

Jesus Christ is also an *heir*. This is one of more than 100 titles given to Him in Scripture. But with Him there is absolutely no restriction or limitation. "Heir of all things" is what God's Word says (see Heb. 1:2). And in the book of Revelation the *through* is expanded: "The kingdom of the world has become the kingdom of our Lord and of His Christ, and he will reign for ever and ever" (Rev. 11:15).

People occasionally challenge the right of an heir or the recipient of a will. They contend, "Why should that other person receive all that he or she has been given?"

Have you ever wondered that about Jesus? There are good reasons why He should receive everything. Read on...

First, He has the right because He is the *Son* of God. "Heir" is a legal term used to denote a person who receives an inheritance by natural right rather than through a will. This right to receive is determined by the bloodline, usually to the nearest of kin. But second, Jesus is also an heir by *divine appointment*. There is no way anyone can contest His right to the inheritance from the Father.

There is a third reason. Jesus has a right to His inheritance because He was involved in the act of creation—He is our *creator*. He was there to bring the world into being. And He had a part in creating you.

But what about Jesus' humanity? Jesus was a man, too. Jesus was "found in appearance as a man" (Phil. 2:8). "Appearance" doesn't just refer to how He looked, but rather the human side of Him. In contrast to His divinity, which came from within, His humanity is assumed from the outside. Jesus was both. If you don't completely understand how this could be, you're not alone.

Keep in mind that the Jesus you follow is not only a man, He is also God. Scripture speaks of this again and again: "In Him all the fullness of the Deity lives in bodily form" (Col. 2:9). "We wait for the blessed hope—the glorious appearing of our great God and Savior, Jesus Christ" (Titus 2:13). Too often what we believe about Jesus is a bit limited.

Do you ever stop to consider that the person you call "Jesus" is God? Maybe that explains the miracles that you still see happening today or the radical transformation of a wasted life into a life that is productive or the comfort you experience when you share your struggles and griefs with Him.

Jesus is different. He is unique. He is special. He is risen and alive. After all, He is God.[1]

QUESTIONS FOR REFLECTION

Who is Jesus in your life? What was your life like without Him? Are you prepared to tell the unsaved people you work and live with about who He is and how He has transformed you? Have you stopped to think about Jesus as God, as the Creator and the only one who can bring life to the dead and wounded places in each one of us? If you have, will you share that new life with someone you work or live with today?

Note
1. Henry Gariepy, *100 Portraits of Christ* (Wheaton, Ill.: Victor Press, 1987), pp. 31-32, 43-44, adapted.

84

On Your Face

*How long, O Lord? Wilt Thou forget me forever? How long
wilt Thou hide Thy face from me?*
—PSALM 13:1

It's one of life's most embarrassing moments. You know that everyone within shouting distance saw it happen. If the ground was soft and pliable, your nose probably made a two- to three-inch indentation (depending on the size of your nose!). If the ground was hard and ungiving, what gave was your nose, and it probably splattered all over your face. But the physical pain wasn't anything compared to the humiliation. You've probably figured out what I'm referring to by now. It's that event in life when you are walking along on perfectly flat ground and for some unknown reason, your feet get tangled, your legs become more horizontal than vertical and before you know it, you are flat on your face. There's no way to hide. It's obvious. And too often this scene happens when you're trying to make a memorable entrance somewhere. This entrance was memorable all right, but not the way you wanted. That's one way to get flat on your face.

Another way is one you've probably seen in movies or on TV. It's where a police officer apprehends someone and tells the person, "Hit the ground and I mean flat on your face!" And the person does so unless he or she has a death wish. That's another way to end up flat on your face. Hopefully you haven't experienced that one.

But there is another way to be flat on your face. Let's look at this way in the life of David, writer of many of the psalms, to see what it is.

In Psalm 13 we find David *flat on his face* because he was despondent. David had experienced so many trials for so long that he was down. He felt abandoned by God. Sound familiar? In *The Living Bible* Psalm 13:1 says, "How long will you look the other way when I am in need?" David had come to the place where he was focusing on his misery. It's easy to do that, just like it's easy to focus on what has gone wrong in your life rather than what you have to be grateful for.

Part of the problem is revealed in verse 2: "How long shall I take counsel in my soul?" David was trying to work out the problem himself, in his own mind, but we see the result of that. He ends up with "having sorrow in my heart all the day." Carrying our burdens by ourselves keeps us flat on our faces.

But David came to his senses. Instead of complaining and berating God, he then said, "Consider and answer me, O Lord, my God; enlighten my eyes" (v. 3). He doesn't see God as distant; he is asking God for the answer.

"Enlighten" means "to cause to shine." David wanted God's brightness to reflect what came from his eyes. David had moved from being flat on his face to being on his knees. Have you been there lately? It's not that uncomfortable. Praying places problems in perspective.

Later in verse 5, we read, "I have trusted in Thy lovingkindness; my heart shall rejoice." In contrast to being on his face, David is now on his feet—moving, rejoicing, delighting in God. Did his circumstances change? No. His position changed: From face to knees to feet.

Read this psalm again. Follow it. After all, a change of position may be all you need.

QUESTIONS FOR REFLECTION

Have you made some embarrassing decisions lately that have left you flat on your face? Are you lying there in despair and humiliation? If so, will you allow the Lord to give you a hand? Why not get on your knees and ask Him to change your focus? Do you believe He can help you get back on your feet? Isn't that where you want to be?

85

Temptation and You

*For we do not have a high priest who cannot sympathize with
our weaknesses, but one who has been tempted in all things
as we are, yet without sin.*

—HEBREWS 4:15

It began in the Garden of Eden with two innocents who became the villains responsible for every calamity that has befallen humanity.

God had given everything in this world to Adam and Eve. He had withheld nothing—except the fruit of a single tree planted in the middle of the Garden.

Satan focused Adam and Eve's minds on God's single restriction and suggested that God was selfish for not giving them everything.

Satan made the forbidden fruit look good, attractive and necessary. And he tried to make God look foolish.

Eve, and then Adam, yielded. They sinned and pulled the whole human race down with them.

Temptation's purpose is to cause us to do what God has told us not to do.

Temptation's strategy is to make wrong look right and bad look good.

Temptation's ultimate goal is to destroy.

There was another young man who faced temptation.

He also was
> young
>> and sensitive
>>> and efficient
>>>> and attentive
>>>>> and far from home
>>>>>> and 30.

He had come to rebuild what Satan had destroyed.

He met the tempter, resisted the temptations and taught us everything we need to know to overcome temptation's power.

He taught us that temptation always strikes in one of three areas:
> the physical
>> the psychological
>>> or the spiritual.

There are some things to remember about temptation.

First, temptation is not a sin (see Jas. 1:14,15).

That's encouraging isn't it? Everywhere we look in this present world, we see something that suggests sin to us. But the suggestion to sin is not the same as sin.

Second, temptation does not come from God (v. 13).

God allows evil, but He never causes it in the lives of His children.

Third, the power to resist temptation comes from God (1 Cor. 10:13):

No temptation has overtaken you but such as is common to man; and God is faithful, who will not allow you to be tempted beyond what you are able, but with the temptation will provide the way of escape also, that you may be able to endure it.

Notice the obvious in this verse. Everybody has the same problem—temptation. But no temptation is greater than the power God has made available to us.

Fourth, the weapons have been provided.

Jesus used Scripture to overcome temptations. So should we. Jesus taught us to pray:

And lead us not into temptation (Luke 11:4).

Pray the words that are part of the model prayer best known to mankind.

James encouraged accountability:

Confess your sins to one another (5:16).

Share your temptation problem with a trusted friend. Ask him or her to...

pray for you
     check up on you
          and be available to you.

We all struggle with our physical appetites. We all want to be some-body. We all tend to create our own gods.

Today's temptations are too great to be endured alone.

Christ provides compassion (see Heb. 4:15).

Believe it or not, Jesus had the same kinds of problems common to all people. That's why the Bible tells us in Hebrews 4:15 that He was tempt-

ed "in all things as we are, yet without sin."
He understands...
  the pressure
    the persistence
      and the pain of being tempted.
He understands the subtle strategies with which Satan attacks us.
He even knows how it feels to crave something we shouldn't have.
And because He knows, He cares.
And because He cares, He helps.
He helps even when He knows how much we want something we shouldn't have.
He helps even when He knows we sometimes don't want His help.[1]

QUESTIONS FOR REFLECTION

What are some of the wrong attitudes and actions Satan has caused you to believe are right? What are some of the pressures you struggle with among your peers? Are you tempted to tackle your pressures alone? What does James 5:16 say about this? He has promised to give you a way of escape, but will you take it?

Note

1. Don Baker, *Lord, I've Got a Problem* (Eugene, Oreg.: Harvest House, 1988), pp. 91-96.

86
Who and What Are Your Idols?

Therefore speak to them and tell them, "Thus says the
Lord God, 'Any man of the house of Israel who sets up
his idols in his heart, puts right before his face the stumbling
block of his iniquity, and then comes to the prophet, I the
Lord will be brought to give him an answer in the matter
in view of the multitude of his idols, in order to lay hold
of the hearts of the house of Israel who are estranged
from Me through all their idols'"

—EZEKIEL 14:4,5

We live in a time in which we create idols. We idolize people: who they are, what they do and their achievements. Sometimes we even confess our idolatry through statements such as: "I really idolize you." But these false idols of our hearts keep us from close relationship with God. And when we idolize someone or something, we often find ourselves in bondage to that person or thing.

We are an independent people today. We don't like being told what to do. But God is still God and He won't accept second place to anything or anyone else. We can't have God as well as other idols.

You may be thinking that you don't worship any other gods or have any other idols. Let's think about some possibilities though. What about the idol of pride? Many today want to be their own god and run their own lives on their own terms. This thinking is a selfish idol that grows and grows until it finally gets us into some kind of deep trouble. It ruins dating relationships as well as friendships and marriages.

It can also be fatal—as a frog found one day. This frog had a problem with envy. It's true! He saw geese flying and envied them so much that he wanted to be like them. One day he talked two geese into putting a strong stick between their beaks. He then told them to fly in close formation with the stick in their mouths. With his mouth, the frog grabbed the stick and the two geese took off. All of a sudden the frog was flying. They cruised though the sky and flew over a small town low enough so the people could see what was happening. The people were amazed. The frog heard them saying, "That's fantastic! A flying frog! Who was the clever one who came up with that ingenious idea?" The frog couldn't resist. He opened his mouth to tell them it was his idea. You know the rest of the story. Pride did this frog in just like it will each of us.

There's another idol that has a close connection to our pride. It's the idol of our pasts. Too many base their significance and value on their past accomplishments. If the present is especially uninteresting or boring, it's easy to fall back on what we did before and make sure everyone is aware of it.

There's another way we idolize the past. It has to do with our experiences with God. We recall the times God worked in our lives, gave us a special experience or empowered us in a new way. Some live so much with their memories that the memories become an idol. They forget Isaiah 43:19: "Behold, I will do a new thing" *(NKJV)*. We are to live expectantly for the future: "'For I know the plans that I have for you,' declares the Lord, 'plans for welfare and not for calamity to give you a future and a hope'" (Jer. 29:11).

Expect God to work in new and better ways for your future. Don't be limited by great experiences in the past.

There are many idols we could examine, but consider just one more—it's the idol of possessions. Our culture preaches possessions, even if you can't afford them. The purpose of advertising today is to make you believe your life will be fulfilled by what you have. As the slogan goes, "Whoever dies with the most toys wins!"[1]

When we idolize money and possessions, we forget who owns what we have. It's not ours—it's God's. Perhaps the best way to remind us of this is through our giving.

QUESTIONS FOR REFLECTION

Are you a flying frog? Have you been trying too hard to get recognition from your family, friends and coworkers? Are you living in the present or have you built an idolatrous shrine around your past victories? Do you have a vision for the future? Is your identity in your things or the God who created all things?

Note
1. Lloyd John Ogilvie, *Conversations with God* (Eugene, Oreg.: Harvest House Publishers, 1992), pp. 31-35, adapted.

87

Are You on Overload?

Come to Me, all who are weary and heavy-laden,
and I will give you rest.
—MATTHEW 11:28

Overloaded? Are there days when you want to throw in the towel? Do you feel wiped out, exhausted, like a two-ton truck that's doing the job of a four-ton truck? Have you ever seen a truck that's been overloaded? It's not a pretty sight. The entire frame begins to sag, the tires flatten and the driver just waits for something else to give. It does.

For the first time in history, we live in an era of overload. Our culture seems to thrive on adding more and more detail to our lives. Perhaps you know about it already. It's the problem of "one more": one more job, one more change, one more activity, one more expectation, one more purchase, one more debt and one more....The load limit has been exceeded. Even in the Church.

Just because you're single, others often think you have more time on your hands to take on even more. If only they knew! Overloading happens when you exceed your physical limits. It happens when you exceed your performance limits. When you do, mistakes are made.

Emotional and mental limits can be exceeded too. Sometimes we quote, "I can do all things through Him who strengthens me" (Phil. 4:13), and use this verse as an excuse to go through life overdoing. But God didn't call us to an unbalanced life. Jesus didn't do it *all*. He didn't heal *all*, visit *all* or teach *all*. Neither can we.

Our culture puts so much pressure on us that we find ourselves making choices about the kinds of overload we will experience. Dr. Richard A. Swenson, M.D. discusses many of them in his insightful book *Margin*. Some of them are listed in the following text so you can choose which of these may fit you:

Have you experienced *activity overload*? You're booked up weeks in advance to the extent that you don't even have any pleasure in anticipating what you're going to do. Where is God's will for you in what you do?

What about *choice overload*? You face this even in the grocery store where you have 24,531 items in the average supermarket.

The person who can't say no encounters *commitment overload*. Often this person's choices are made out of the fear of rejection: *What would others think if I said no?*

Have you encountered the *hurry overload* syndrome yet? Did God create hurry? If not, who did? Do you ever hear yourself saying, *I need to run?* The hurry-up tendency creeps into the glossary of our everyday language. When do you find yourself hurrying? Some will say all the time.

How about *debt overload?* It's hard to find anyone anymore who is out of debt. But when it hangs over our heads, it's a distraction from the rest of life's activities.

A major overload which is getting worse each day is *noise overload*. You can't even go into a nice restaurant for a quiet meal without having to compete with music blaring over a speaker. Can you handle quiet? Can you feel comfortable without the radio or TV on?

Perhaps we need to program nonactivities and quiet times into our lives each day. If we don't, how else can we begin to experience what the Psalmist said, "Be still and know that I am God" (Ps. 46:10, *NIV*)?

Where do you feel overloaded? Identify it, correct it and become different from others. Too much of anything is just that—too much—with one exception: Our relationship with the Lord. There's never too much of that. He's the one who can restore a balance to our lives.[1]

QUESTIONS FOR REFLECTION

Which of the major overloads keep your life unbalanced? Do you tend to overload yourself more physically, emotionally or mentally? Is this because you are trying to fill some deep hunger that only God's love can fill? Will you trust Him to fill the empty places in you today?

Note
1. Richard A. Swenson, M.D., *Margin* (Colorado Springs: NavPress, 1992), pp. 74-84, adapted.

88

Be Careful Out There

Therefore let him who thinks he stands take heed lest he fall.
—1 CORINTHIANS 10:12

For a number of years television viewers were captivated by the action-packed police show *Hill Street Blues*. The offices at this precinct were occupied by a varied and even motley group of characters. In fact, you weren't sure as a viewer if you'd even want to call some of them to help you!

Each day a morning briefing took place, which was often chaotic and even disruptive. But just before these rowdy characters were dismissed, the sergeant would pause and then say to the police officers, "Let's be careful out there!" He was warning them to be on the alert, to keep their guards up and to never slack off because the unpredictable could and would happen.

The same advice is given to boxers. The trainer will tell the fighter: "Keep your guard up. If you don't, you'll get knocked out!"

Basketball coaches can be seen yelling at their players to keep their hands up and keep moving to protect their goals.

It's good advice for police officers and athletes.

It's good advice for us as well.

You are faced with a number of issues in this world that are just begging you to leave behind your Christian values and standards. It's tough being single and the only Christian where you work or in the apartment complex where you live. There can be a tendency to slack off when you're with your non-Christian friends or your roommate. Some of the temptations they use to lure you are very enticing—especially when you fail to consider the consequences.

Scripture warns us again and again to "be on your guard." Be on your guard, Jesus said, against hypocrisy (see Matt. 16:6-12); against greed (see Luke 12:15); against persecution from others (see Matt. 10:17); against false teaching (see Mark 13:22,23); and above all, against spiritual slackness and unreadiness for the Lord's return (see Mark 13:32-37). "Be careful," He said in Luke 21:34, *(NIV)*, or your hearts will be weighed down with dissipation, drunkenness and the anxieties of life. To "be careful" means to be wary, to keep your eyes open, to be alert.

It only takes one time of letting your guard down and the worst can happen. What do others remember? All the times you kept your guard up or the one time you let it down? You know the answer.

That is why the same caution is repeated throughout the Scriptures. Listen to these warnings in the *New International Version*: "Only be careful, and watch yourselves" (Deut. 4:9). "Be careful to do what the Lord your God has commanded you" (Deut. 5:32). "Be careful that you do not forget the Lord" (Deut. 6:12). "Be careful to obey all that is written in the Book" (Josh. 23:6). "Give careful thought to your ways" (Hag. 1:5-7). "Be careful to do what is right" (Rom. 12:17). "Be careful that you don't fall" (1 Cor. 10:12). "Be careful, then, how you live" (Eph. 5:15). "Be careful that none of you be found to have fallen short" (Heb. 4:1).

Where is it that you need to exercise the most caution? Who are the people you need be most careful around?

Remember, there's a reason for all the warnings. We need to be reminded of them constantly. If you're struggling with an issue, read these passages out loud every morning for a month. Before long you will know them from memory. That's the best safeguard.[1]

QUESTIONS FOR REFLECTION

Are you working in an office with a motley crew? What steps have you taken to keep up your guard and protect your physical, emotional and spiritual life in that place? Are you careful about those you choose to date? What about the people with whom you socialize? Would God be honored by your relationships? If not, what steps will you take to "be careful"?

Note
1. Gary Rosberg, *Guard Your Heart* (Portland, Oreg.: Multnomah, 1994), pp. 15-17, adapted.

So You've Got an Attitude—Don't We All!

*Have this attitude in yourselves which
was also in Christ Jesus.*

—PHILIPPIANS 2:5

You've heard it and you've probably said it about someone: "Do *they* ever have an attitude!" That's not really a compliment, is it? It's more of a warning to others.

And it's not just people who have "attitudes" either. Animals can also have them, especially...cats. They seem to be born with attitude problems. If you've spent much time around them, you've seen it. Usually the attitude is "Don't bother me. I'll get back to you when I'm good and ready." It's a sign of independence and a "better than you" attitude. No wonder dogs love to chase them!

Do you know what attitude is? It's an inner feeling or viewpoint that is evident by behavior. And no words have to be spoken to express this—it's seen in the way people walk into the room or pout or stick out the jaw or...you can probably think of some other expressions.

Did you know that airplanes can have attitudes? It's true! According to John Maxwell and one of his experiences in a small plane, there is a small-gadget instrument panel that's an attitude indicator. The attitude of a plane is the position of the aircraft in relation to the horizon. When the plane is climbing, it has a nose-high attitude because the nose of the plane is pointed above the horizon. And when the plane is diving, that's a nose-down attitude. And since the attitude of a plane determines its performance, flight instructors now teach attitude flying. Isn't that interesting? It's not much different with people. Our attitude definitely affects how we respond. If you want to see an example of a healthy attitude look at Jesus.

He wasn't just concerned about Himself. He was others-centered rather than self-centered:

Do nothing from selfishness or empty conceit, but with humility of mind let each of you regard one another as more important than himself; do not merely look out for your own personal interests, but also for the interests of others (Phil. 2:3,4).

He was also a secure person. He wasn't driven by fear or insecurities. Just the opposite:

Who, although He existed in the form of God, did not regard equality with God a thing to be grasped, but emptied Himself, taking the form of a bond-servant, and being made in the likeness of men (Phil. 2:6,7).

He was submissive:

And being found in appearance as a man, He humbled Himself by becoming obedient to the point of death, even death on a cross (Phil. 2:8).

Did you know that your attitude is more important than your IQ? Did you know that your attitude is more important than your appearance? Did you know that your attitude is more important than what you're worth? You can be tops in these areas and get nowhere because of your attitude. Your attitude is like a thermostat. It will determine whether you succeed or fail. Your attitude will:

- Determine your approach to life. Do you see the positive, the possible, the potential or the negative?
- Determine your relationships with people. Unhealthy attitudes cripple work relationships as well as promotions.
- Determine the outcome of a task more than anything else. You get what you were looking for. Remember the difference between buzzards and bees. Buzzards search for food by flying around and looking for dead animals. When they find the smelly, fly-ridden, decaying animals, they move in to gorge. Honey bees have different habits. They look for the nectar which is sweet. They're very discriminating as they fly through the garden. Both the bees and buzzards find what they are seeking.

So does a positive and a negative attitude find what it's seeking? Some people don't need a heart transplant, they need an attitude transplant.

And thank God, it's easier to get a new attitude than a new heart. How's your attitude today? Use the scriptures in Philippians 2 as your model.[1]

QUESTIONS FOR REFLECTION

What is your attitude toward your job, the people you work with, the opportunities you do or do not have, your church, your neighbor, the world you live in and those you are forced to share the planet with each day? What changes do you need to make to develop the qualities that Jesus modeled? Are you a buzzard or a bee?

Note
1. John C. Maxwell, *The Winning Attitude* (Nashville: Thomas Nelson, 1993), pp. 1-29, adapted.

A Prayer for Today

*So I say live by the Spirit, and you will not gratify the
desires of the sinful nature. For the sinful nature desires what
is contrary to the Spirit, and the Spirit what is contrary to the
sinful nature. They are in conflict with each other,
so that you do not do what you want. But if you are
led by the Spirit, you are not under law.*
—GALATIANS 5:16-18 *(NIV)*

Lord,

You have given me everything good in my life. Remind me that I haven't done it and that I'm not You. I pray now for a greater sense of responsibility.

I praise You for understanding me and my struggles. I admit that I have numerous faults that still interfere with living my life as You want. Forgive me for my conscious and purposeful acts of sin, as well as those that seem to creep in even though I'm fighting against them.

Help me to remember my sense of responsibility to myself.

Help me never to do anything so I lose my self-respect.

Help me to accept and rejoice in my status whether it is to be single temporarily or permanently.

Help me never to let myself down by doing anything that attacks or destroys another person.

Help me never to do anything that I would spend the rest of my life regretting.

Help me not to say one thing with my words and another with my actions.

Help me not to criticize others for the same faults I see in myself.

Help me not to demand standards from others that I make little or no effort to fulfill.

Help me not to play and skirt around temptations that I know are my weakness.

Help me to deal with the inability to say yes or no and to be definite in my commitments.

Help me with my stubbornness and reluctance to give up habits that I know are wrong and break my relationship with You.

Help me to quit trying to please both worlds; forgive me for pleasing others and myself first rather than You.

Lord, I want to always remember my responsibility to my friends, to those I love, and to those who love me and those who don't.

I want to be faithful so I don't disappoint those who love me.

Help me not to fail anyone who depends on me.

Keep me from being a source of grief to others.

Lord, sometimes it's difficult to be faithful, but I know that You can keep me faithful. Thank You that it's not just up to me!

Help me not to be one who remembers my rights and forgets my responsibilities.

Help me not to be one who wants to get everything out of life without putting anything into it.

Help me not to be one who doesn't care what happens to others.

Remind me that I am responsible to You and will answer to You for the way I use what You have given me.

And help me each minute of the day to remember how much You love me and how Jesus died for me. I praise You.

Thank You for hearing, for responding, and for working in my life. In Jesus' name,

Amen.[1]

QUESTIONS FOR REFLECTION

Does this prayer reflect the attitude of your heart? If so, what steps are you willing to take today to live a life that is more fully devoted to Him? Does your life reflect a single purpose?

Note

1. William Barclay, *A Barclay Prayer Book* (London: SCM Press Ltd., 1963), pp. 248-249, 254-255, adapted.